Because
INDIA
COMES FIRST

Ram Madhav is an Indian politician, social leader, author and thinker. Dr Madhav is the president of India Foundation, a New Delhi-based think tank. He has served as the National General Secretary of the Bharatiya Janata Party during 2014–20 responsible for handling the political affairs of Jammu & Kashmir, Assam and other northeastern states of India.

Dr Madhav has over 300 publications to his credit. He has authored several books in English and Telugu, which include *The Hindutva Paradigm: Integral Humanism and the Quest for a Non-Western Worldview* and *Uneasy Neighbours: India and China after 50 Years of the War*.

He is a regular contributor to platforms like *The Indian Express*, *The Hindustan Times* and *OPEN magazine* amongst others. He was the editor of *Bharatiya Pragna*, a monthly magazine published in English by Pragna Bharati, and associate editor of *Jagriti*, a Telugu weekly.

Because
INDIA
COMES FIRST

REFLECTIONS ON NATIONALISM,
IDENTITY AND CULTURE

RAM MADHAV

Published by
Rupa Publications India Pvt. Ltd 2024
7/16, Ansari Road, Daryaganj
New Delhi 110002

Sales centres:
Bengaluru Chenna Hyderabad
Jaipur Kathmandu Kolkata
Mumbai Prayagraj

Copyright © Ram Madhav 2020, 2024

First published by Westland Publications Private Limited 2020

The views and opinions expressed in this book are the author's own and the facts are as reported by him which have been verified to the extent possible, and the publishers are not in any way liable for the same.

All rights reserved.
No part of this publication may be reproduced, transmitted, or stored in a retrieval system, in any form or by any means, electronic, mechanical, photocopying, recording or otherwise, without the prior permission of the publisher.

P-ISBN: 978-81-969113-1-7
E-ISBN: 978-81-969113-5-5

First impression 2024

10 9 8 7 6 5 4 3 2 1

The moral right of the author has been asserted.

Printed in India

This book is sold subject to the condition that it shall not, by way of trade or otherwise, be lent, resold, hired out, or otherwise circulated, without the publisher's prior consent, in any form of binding or cover other than that in which it is published.

Contents

Introduction ix

The Spirit of Democracy

1. The Art of the Possible — 3
2. A Study in Greatness — 7
3. On Gandhi and Gandhism — 14
4. The Beauty of Indic Thought — 22
5. Three Warnings of B.R. Ambedkar — 27
6. Cultivating Constitutional Morality — 35
7. Samajik Samrasta (Social Harmony): Shri Guruji M.S. Golwalkar — 40
8. Deendayal Upadhyaya: The Swayamsewak — 47
9. Betrayal of the Mahatama — 51
10. A Need for Vigilance — 55

Confronting History

11. Correcting a Historic Blunder — 61
12. Kashmir: The End of Victimhood Politics — 65
13. Kashmir is Ours, Also Means That Every Kashmiri is Ours — 82
14. Are Gupkaris Listening? — 86

15.	A Time for New Leaders	90
16.	The Supremacy of the Indian State and Parliament	94
17.	Roots and Rights in Assam after NRC	97
18.	A Different Leader	105
19.	A People's Idea	109
20.	Strategic Culture	113

A View from Within

21.	Gentle, Yet Atal	119
22.	In Atalji's Mould	125
23.	Election Result: In Favour of Narendra Modi	129
24.	Glasnost in RSS	134
25.	Leader, Cadre, Parivar	138
26.	Ram Mandir Movement: A One-Way Street for BJP	142
27.	Somnath to Ayodhya: Journey of an Awakened Civilisation	146
28.	Ayodhya is for Ayuddha: Non-War and Peace Communities	150
29.	In Sita's Footsteps	154
30.	Despite the People	161
31.	After Empowerment, Freedom and Dignity	165
32.	Because India Comes First	169

Facing the Facts

33.	Liberal Fascists	175
34.	Know Your Terrorist	178

35.	Citizenship Act: For Persecuted Minorities	183
36.	At the Root of Today's Crisis, an Intellectual Void	190
37.	Our Lives Matter	194
38.	Soft Power Struggles	199
39.	Challenges to Global Governance	203
40.	When Democracy was Unshackled	207

India and the World

41.	Shalom Al Yisrael	213
42.	Look beyond Transactionalism	220
43.	Maa Ganga by Another Name	224
44.	The Meaning of De-hyphenation	229
45.	Turning down China	233
46.	New India, Different China	237
47.	Wolf Warrior Diplomacy	241
48.	The Heat in Beijing	245
49.	Going beyond Panchsheel	251
50.	China: The Real Foreign Policy Challenge for India	256
51.	India has a Moral Commitment on Tibet	260
52.	The Dalai Lama at Eighty-Five	271
53.	COVID-19 and the Contours of the New World Order	277

Acknowledgements   281

Introduction

India fascinated many. One unbroken civilisation that has lived on for millennia and made its mark globally through numerous significant interventions over an uninterrupted history, the India story has been told and retold a number of times by those charmed by its grace and grandeur. Through its living history of over five millennia, India has offered invaluable gems of wisdom, enriching all of mankind.

Etat Desha Prasutasya Sakashat Agrajanmanah
Swam Swam Charitram Siksheran Prithivyam Sarv Manavah

This was proclaimed in *Manusmriti*, one of the oldest constitutions of India. It means, 'Men all over the world would come to beseech lessons in character through the lives of the great men born in this country.'

'We owe a lot to India,' declared the renowned scientist Albert Einstein. For Mark Twain, the celebrated American author and humourist, India was the cradle of the human race. French philosopher Roman Rolland described India as that place on earth where the living dreams of all men have found their home. Martin Luther King Jr insisted that a visit to India was not just tourism but a pilgrimage. The greatest tribute came from the renowned German scholar and Orientalist, Max Mueller. 'If I were asked under what sky the human mind has most fully developed some of its choicest gifts, has most deeply pondered on the greatest problems of life, and has found solutions, I should point to India,' Mueller mused, capturing the immense contribution that India has made to the world of ideas.

The India story is about transformative and civilising ideas. The West took several millennia to come to terms with certain ideas like virtue, liberty and reason that define human existence. The journey of Western thought began several millennia ago in the Greek city-states of Athens and Sparta. Building a virtuous man and a virtuous society preoccupied the thoughts of the early European thinkers. The Romans, having taken over the empires, also reigned over the kingdom of ideas. The religions of the Jews and the Christians insisted that belief in God is the only recourse for man to become virtuous. But the Roman kings insisted on their own divine authority. The Enlightenment thinkers, after the era of Reformation, started challenging the notion of religious supremacy and argued in favour of man's ability to think for himself and the community. Reason, thus, came to occupy centre stage in the Western worldview. However, the struggle between religion and reason continues to remain unresolved to this day in the West.

India, on the other hand, resolved this fundamental dilemma at the very beginning of its civilisational journey by declaring, in the world-renowned Hindu monk Swami Vivekananda's words, that 'every individual soul' is 'potentially divine'. The man versus God discourse was, therefore, always alien to the Indian genius. Having resolved the most complex cobwebs of human thinking about existence, its purpose and the ultimate reality—the *telos* of

Greek discourse—early on, through the scholarly debates in the Vedas, Indian thought set out on the journey of enlightening and ennobling the human race through the doctrine of *'Krinvanto Vishwam Aryam'* (Make the world noble).

Unlike the Greeks and Romans, or the yesteryear colonisers of the West, the India story is not about kings and kingdoms, wars and conquests, barbarity and slavery. It is about carrying the message of human freedom, human dignity and human virtue to all corners of the human heart. India conquered lands and hearts through its uplifting ideas and values. It enriched its own national society through the righteous code called Dharma—the essence of wisdom accumulated over millennia over intense dialogues and discourses held by mendicants and meditators, saints and savants, and the wise among the citizenry.

Dharma in India is the epitome of everything, from individual life to collective action, from a local ritual to the grandiose festival, from cuisine to costume, from the innocence of a local dialect to the grandiloquence of its great languages. India's social life and political values too were shaped by the profound and pristine essence of Dharma. In a nutshell, Vivekananda admired India as the *'Dharma Prana Bharata'*, the country with Dharma as the soul or life force.

It is this India story, a story of enriching wisdom and ennobling ideas, which manifests all through its history from Ram and Krishna to Shivaji and Rana Pratap; through its spirituality from Vyasa and Valmiki to Aurobindo, Dayananda and Vivekananda; through its political thought from Bhishma, Parashara and Manu to Gandhi, Lohia, Deendayal Upadhyaya and Ambedkar.

While it was home to the world's most treasured ideas and ideals, India's doors were never shut to the wisdom emanating from elsewhere in the world. When modern Western thinking produced ideas like socialism, secularism, human rights and democracy, India received them with open arms. It internalised them so eloquently because the core values behind those newly framed Western ideas gelled effectively with ancient Indian thought and institutions. Ram Rajya, the favourite ideal of Gandhi and many other visionaries of India, was essentially about a statecraft centred on the will and wisdom of the people, their rights and responsibilities.

The essays in this book, written over many years, represent that story of India. Decades of learning through contact with wise men and institutions has helped me shape and structure my thoughts, which gushed out through my pen in the form of these articles. The essence of that learning has been captured in the title of this book: *Because India Comes First*.

THE SPIRIT OF DEMOCRACY

'Republics are created by the virtue, public spirit, and intelligence of the citizens. They fall, when the wise are banished from the public councils, because they dare to be honest, and the profligate are rewarded, because they flatter the people in order to betray them.'

—Joseph Story

1

The Art of the Possible

As a non-political young activist, I used to abhor phrases like 'politics is the art of the possible'. I used to think that it is rank opportunism to think that way. This is because in the RSS, I had been trained to believe that it is ideology that should guide us at every level, and the ideology is always in black and white. Four years into political activism, I now realise that the statement is probably true in the present-day milieu of politics. Politics has today become an art that requires skillful handling. It is not a 'political science'; it is the 'art of politics' today.

Conventional politics is a leveller. All political parties practise it, and many have mastery over it. Appeals to caste, creed, state, sex, race and religion form part of it. Money and muscle power are integral to it. Fiery political speeches often filled with lies and innuendos; targeting the ruling establishment with a singularly negative campaign and looking for potential trouble spots are the stock-in-trade of opposition parties, while ruling parties retaliate by resorting to populist schemes and the misuse of official mechanisms.

All these are perils of democratic systems. 'Democracy is the second best form of governance. The best form is yet to be invented,' commented a political scientist. It is nobody's case that democracies are perfect systems. As Fareed Zakaria points out in his book, *The Future of Freedom*, there are democracies that can be described as 'illiberal' all over the world, while there are non-democratic or semi-democratic governments that are seen as benevolent and liked by their people.

Take the case of countries in the Middle East. Most of them are ruled by autocratic regimes. Give them democracy, and some of them may end up posthumously electing Osama bin Laden as their leader. On the other hand, there are countries like Bhutan, Brunei and the UAE where democracies are either very nascent or non-existent. Yet people in all those countries seem to be happy with their regimes. Even in countries like Singapore under Lee Kuan Yew or Indonesia under Sukarno, it was an authoritarian form of democracy that was in vogue for many decades, largely liked by the people.

In essence, it is not so much about the form, but about the quality of the subjects, the people. Gandhiji used to fear that in a country like India with large-scale illiteracy and backwardness, there is a danger of democracy degenerating into mobocracy. It is not an imagined fear. The mob's mind can't be a rational mind. We have seen the catastrophic consequences of it in history. It shouldn't be forgotten that even Hitler was elected through a popular democratic mandate.

When such situations arise, it is tempting to become rhetorical by resorting to clichés like, 'A society gets a government it deserves.' This may be true. Because that is how democracies function. It is the rule of the majority; moreover, there is no clear definition of a 'majority'; hence the right description is that 'it is the rule of first-past-the-post'.

The success of democracies lies in improving the quality of their citizens and as a consequence the quality of their representatives. Joseph Story, an eminent jurist and Congressman of the United States of America, had once wryly observed, 'Republics are created by the virtue, public spirit and intelligence of the citizens. They fall, when the wise are banished from the public councils, because they dare to be honest, and the profligate are rewarded, because they flatter the people, in order to betray them.'

When democracies fail because of their people and leaders, what is the remedy? Apoptosis? Like Kamikaze pilots, do we expect failed democracies to self-destruct? The answer is 'no'. What we need is leaders who can continually reform and improve our democratic institutions.

Indians have never accepted the proposition, 'A society gets a government it deserves.' Instead, Indians believe '*Rajah Kaalasya Kaaranam*': the ruler is responsible for the times. Hence, he must reign over and mould it as per his wishes.

Democracies thrive on the strength of several institutions. Leadership of each institution is responsible for upholding the dignity of democracy. People, politicians, the judiciary and the administration, all have distinct yet complementary roles that ensure democracy's success. If one institution shirks its responsibility, democracy is weakened to that extent.

The role of the judiciary is even more important since it enjoys utmost power as well as utmost freedom. In fact, in India today, the judiciary is seen by many as the highest beacon of hope. But then, it too has a hierarchy and this determines whether the much-adored institution will live up to expectations.

In India, the judiciary is passing through a rigorous test on this account. Some of its recent judgments have invited the serious attention of lay people and pundits alike. The Sabarimala verdict is one such case in question; so is the apex court's reluctance to take up the Ram Janmabhoomi matter. There is a conspicuous disconnect between the views of people at large and judges on the court benches.

Democracy, rule of law, peace and public order are not just the responsibility of the political establishment alone; they need the support of other organs of the state, especially the judiciary. Only then can the political establishment deliver and democracies flourish. When all institutions are functional, then will public affairs be a 'political science'. Else, politicians will resort to what we call the 'art of politics', a phrase with many meanings, some beneficent but some others potentially damaging.

2

A Study in Greatness

Two great men belonging to two successive generations have revolutionised world politics in the last century. As their influence went far beyond the countries they were from and spread all over the world in the past five decades, they became an inspiration to the struggles of oppressed people everywhere. They were Gandhi and Mandela: the Mahatma and Madiba. This year happens to be the 150th birth anniversary of Gandhi and the birth centenary of Mandela.

The two never met. When Gandhi died in 1948, Nelson Mandela was a budding leader in South Africa, starting off with little that Gandhi had lived and died for. But then Gandhi transformed Mandela. It was one of Gandhi's biographies that Mandela came across during his long years in jail that turned South Africa's one-time Marxist into a messiah of peace and non-violence.

During his lifetime, Gandhi had inspired thousands in India to adopt his path and work at mitigating the trials and tribulations of millions of citizens of this country. A single meeting with Gandhi would transform countless youngsters into Gandhians, ready to dedicate their lives to serving the poor. Such true Gandhians can still be found, not in the urban political landscape of India, but among the deprived in remote villages and forest habitations.

Like Gandhi, Mandela also had extraordinary charisma and a unique way to harness the power of people. Wherever the downtrodden discover their voice, we find such a leader as their inspiration. As Barack Obama, the first African-American to rise to the presidency of the United States, once said: 'In my life, I have always looked to Mahatma Gandhi as an inspiration, because he embodies the kind of transformational change that can be made when ordinary people come together to do extraordinary things.' Obama added, 'I believe in Nelson Mandela's vision. I believe in a vision shared by Gandhi and King and Abraham Lincoln. I believe in a vision of equality, justice, freedom, and multi-racial democracy, built on the premise that all people are created equal. We have to follow Madiba's example of persistence and of hope.'

Gandhi and Mandela were born to relatively well-off families. Gandhi's father was a Diwan (minister) in Gujarat, while Mandela's family led a large clan in South Africa. Both had the benefit of a modern education and acquired law degrees. Neither chose to pursue lucre. Instead, they put themselves at the service of a cause. Even in their practice as lawyers, their approach was to aim for reconciliation rather than victory. Gandhi's case was curious. He went to South Africa to fight a legal battle for an Indian immigrant there. The racial discrimination and abuse he had to endure taught him his first lessons in non-violence. For a long time he only fought for Indians, growing conscious of native rights much later; but when he embraced the cause of Black Africans, he firmly declared: 'This land is theirs by birth.'

Similarly, Madiba had initially refrained from including Indians in his struggle, perhaps because of their image as a merchant class exploiting locals. But as his understanding grew, like Gandhi, he broadened his efforts and began to speak on behalf of all those in need of self-determination.

It was in South Africa, defending the fundamental rights of non-Whites to life and dignity, that Gandhi invented his weapon of Satyagraha, which he used so effectively in his fight against the British Raj. Thus, South Africa was the 'karma bhumi'—land of karma—for both Gandhi and Mandela. Mandela once said that while India was Gandhi's motherland, South Africa was the Indian leader's adopted land. 'The Mahatma is an integral part of our history because it is here that he first experimented with truth; here that he demonstrated his characteristic firmness in pursuit of justice; here that he developed Satyagraha as a philosophy and a method of struggle,' he said. 'If Gandhi is the Father of Indian nation, he is the grandfather of South Africa,' commented a former South African diplomat.

The two leaders were unique in their own ways. But Gandhi was a phenomenon. Albert Einstein once observed that 'Generations to come will scarcely believe that such a one as this ever in flesh and blood walked upon this earth.'

They both lived transparent lives. Both spent long years in prison in their countries. Both practised a form of politics that didn't have any place for rancour or retribution and strived to build inclusive societies. At the height of the agitation against the British, Gandhi wouldn't hesitate to call the countrymen to support them during World War II. Mandela even agreed to share his Nobel Peace Prize with the leader of his country's tormentors, F.W. de Klerk.

Gandhi and Mandela were both strong-willed leaders. They fought for truth and fairness in public life. For Gandhi, truth and non-violence was the mantra, while for Mandela truth and reconciliation was the way.

For Gandhi as well as for Mandela, the exalted goal of independence or self-rule was not merely a political struggle, but an inner spiritual journey. It is what led them to dedicate their lives and politics to those at the bottom of the pyramid. They sought to become one with the masses and live among them. Both led simple lives and did not shy away from manual labour. They didn't just preach, they lived out their ideals.

'Mahatma Gandhi came and stood at the door of India's destitute millions, clad as one of themselves, speaking to them in their language … who else has so unreservedly accepted the vast masses of the Indian people as his flesh and blood. Truth awakened Truth,' wrote Rabindranath Tagore. Once Gandhi returned to India in 1914, he gave up Western attire, opted to wear just a loin cloth and join the country's teeming millions in their huts. This led to some consternation in his social circles. Some from his caste even sought to ostracise him from their midst. But nothing would deter Gandhi from his life mission.

'I will give you a talisman,' Gandhi told his followers, 'Whenever you are in doubt or when the self becomes too much with you, apply the following test: Recall the face of the poorest and the weakest man whom you may have seen and ask yourself if the step you contemplate is going to be of any use to him. Will he gain anything by it? Will it restore him to a control over his own life and destiny? In other words, will it lead to Swaraj for the hungry and spiritually starving millions? Then you will find your doubts and your self melting away.'

Mandela had similar principles. 'There is nothing I fear more than waking up without a programme that will help me bring a little happiness to those with no resources, those who are poor, illiterate, and ridden with terminal disease,' he declared. Like Gandhiji, he believed that alleviation of poverty is not a matter of charity but of justice, because poverty is not natural, it's man-made.

One important contribution of these two leaders was that their efforts contained the spread of ideologies like Communism and helped people resist materialism. Gandhi blocked a Communist takeover of the Congress-led independence struggle. Mandela, who was influenced by Marxism in the initial years, later realised its futility. He rejected an armed rebellion in favour of a peaceful struggle.

Since both Gandhi and Mandela pursued unconventional politics, they had many critics and sceptics. Disagreements over their policies and positions continue to this day, but their contributions are no less significant. During India's freedom struggle, well-known critics of his non-violence included Subhas Chandra Bose, who later formed the Azad Hind Fauj and led an armed rebellion against the British. A less known critic of Gandhi's policies was his chosen heir, Jawaharlal Nehru. Nehru categorically rejected Gandhi's ideas put out in Hind Swaraj advocating a village-centric development agenda for India. The differences became so acute that at one point Gandhi is recorded to have said, 'Jawaharlal says he doesn't understand my language. My language is foreign to him. But language is never a barrier in the union of hearts; when I am gone he will speak my language.'

In a letter to Nehru on 5 October 1945, Gandhi writes: 'The first thing I want to write about is the difference in outlook between us. If the difference is fundamental then I feel the public should also be made aware of it. It would be detrimental to our work for Swaraj to keep them in dark.' In Nehru's reply of 9 October 1945, he says: 'I do not understand why a village should necessarily embody truth and non-violence. A village, normally speaking, is backward intellectually and culturally and no progress can be made from a backward environment. Narrow-minded people are much more likely to be untruthful and violent.'

Mandela also had close critics, some from within his immediate family. Winnie Mandela, his wife, was against his adoption of Gandhian methods to fight racism. The couple's views diverged when he was in jail and their differences eventually led to their divorce. Winnie publicly contradicted Nelson Mandel at an event in Germany, repudiating his call to the people of KwaZulu-Natal to throw their weapons into the sea. The way forward, for Winnie, was an armed struggle. She went to the extent of refusing to recognise the leadership of the African National Congress, Mandela's party.

A part of their greatness lay in their openness to criticism and their steadfastness of vision. It is this politics of transparency that is missing today. Thanks to the efforts of Gandhi and Mandela, untouchability and apartheid among people became history, but the new ill of political untouchability has surfaced. Hate has taken over political relations. Tolerance of criticism and of different viewpoints is what the world needs to re-learn from these two great leaders.

Gandhi himself was the architect of his approach, be it non-violence or Satyagraha. Mandela was lucky to have a Gandhi and a Martin Luther King Jr before him. However, where Gandhi ultimately failed to prevent the partition of India, Mandela succeeded in keeping his country united, thanks largely to the lessons learnt from his predecessors.

In a world trapped in a narrative shaped by material realities, Madiba and the Mahatma should awaken us to a deeper truth that comes not merely through political and economic programmes, but spiritual activity steeped in humane ideals and traditions. It's their common values, their belief in introspective prayer, and their faith in the goodness of all creation that give both Gandhi and Mandela an influence that will last forever.

3

On Gandhi and Gandhism

Mahatma Gandhi is a leader who sparks so much passion and attracts so much attention even after 150 years of his birth and 71 years after demise. There are many who love and admire him; there are many for whom he is the political capital; there are some who hate him. You can love him, pretend to love him or hate him—but you can't ignore him. 'I am not going to keep quiet even after I die'—Gandhiji declared gleefully once long ago. He was right.

Mahatma Gandhi was Asia's greatest contribution to the world in the last century. His Ahimsa and Satyagraha—Non-violence and Truthful Resistance—were the only original political programmes that any leader had offered in the last century. After Gandhi's successful experimentation with those programmes in India, they became the essential modus operandi in almost all the struggles for freedom and independence that shook the world in last 70 years and freed people in over 50 countries from the yoke of dictatorships and monarchies. Except for a few countries in Eastern Europe and East Asia that had witnessed violent communist revolutions, all the other countries that have transformed into democracies, had imprints of Gandhian ideals of non-violence and peace in their transformation.

Gandhi had inspired countless leaders, not only in India, but all over the world. What is common among Dominique Pire, a Belgian priest; Adolfo Pérez Esquivel, a teacher in Argentina; Martin Luther King Jr, a civil rights activist in the US; and Nelson Mandela, a freedom fighter in South Africa? All four were Nobel Peace Prize winners. And more importantly, all four had claimed that Mahatma Gandhi was the inspiration for them. India has produced a couple of Nobel laureates, but Gandhi had produced more of them through his ideals. Gandhi continues to inspire countless social activists to this day. There are many Gandhians working silently below the radar in remote far-flung areas among the tribals, scheduled castes and other underprivileged sections of the society.

Today, there are many who swear by Gandhi; but many who hate him too. Churchill hated Gandhi and called him a 'half-naked fakir' and bristled at the very idea of him climbing up the steps of the Buckingham Palace to sit face-to-face with the British monarch. But there Gandhi was, in his same loin cloth, nonchalant about criticism from the highest quarters. When someone asked him if his dress was appropriate for the occasion, Gandhi's reply was that 'the King had enough clothes for both of us'.

One quality that distinguished Gandhi from others was his fearlessness. He never bothered about political correctness, et cetera. This quality was a product of his absolute commitment to truth. 'The essence of his teaching was fearlessness and truth. The voice was something different from others. It was quiet and low, and yet it could be heard above the shouting of the multitude. Behind the language of peace and friendship, there was power and a determination not to submit to the wrong,' said Nehru once.

Gandhians of today can be angry, harsh and unreasonably critical. But Gandhi was not. In his lifetime, he had endured great criticisms and ridicule. Yet, he never tried to give them back. He used to take criticism and ridicule in his stride and move on. 'If I had no sense of humour, I would long ago have committed suicide,' he wrote in 1928 adding, 'Nobody can hurt me without my permission.'

Gandhi was betrayed by many. Godse was one of them. Gandhi had a premonition about the impending death. He talked about it dozens of times in January 1948; but steadfastly refused to take security. For him, accepting security meant deviating from his commitment to non-violence. 'People called me Bapu—a father. If my children want to kill me, so be it,' he would argue. Godse stood in front of him with folded hands, called him 'Bapu' and said 'namaste'; but the next moment, Gandhi's two 'walking sticks', Manu and Abha, were on the ground. Godse had pumped bullets into Gandhi's chest.

Gandhi was betrayed by Godse and his men; but Gandhism was betrayed by Gandhi's own followers. Gandhi is for many a political expediency, and Gandhism just a facade. Gandhism doesn't lie in mechanically rotating the spinning wheel or wearing khadi for public display. 'If Gandhism means simply mechanically turning the spinning wheel, it deserves to be destroyed,' Gandhi had himself declared. Gandhism is about truth, transparency, non-violence, openness to criticism, fearlessness, rejection of political correctness and image consciousness.

Gandhi was accused of harshness towards his wife Kasturba and other members in the family. Historians tell stories about his harsh treatment of them occasionally. But that was partly also because Gandhi didn't just preach ideals but wanted to live up to them. Unlike today's leaders who want others to sacrifice for them while their children and siblings enjoy the fruits of the sacrifices of the others, Gandhi wanted reform to begin at home. When he decided to fight against manual scavenging, he wanted it to start from his family. He asked Kasturba to clean up the toilets. Coming from a traditional and orthodox family, Kasturba, also referred to as 'Ba' (mother), didn't immediately internalise it. Gandhi was angry. But Ba told him that she needed time to understand and follow his philosophy. And she did. There she was, in subsequent struggles of Gandhi, always by his side. She would campaign on his behalf alone on occasions when Gandhi was not available due to incarcerations or ill-health. She went even to Kerala alone to campaign for Harijan Sevak Sangh.

Gandhi's life was dedicated to the uplift of the downtrodden. He started Harijan Sevak Sangh and fought against caste discrimination and untouchability. After returning from London after acquiring a barrister degree, unlike his bete noir Jinnah, Gandhi decided not to start legal practice. He instead chose to live among the poorest of the poor people. Jamnalal Bajaj had donated a piece of land in remote forests near Wardha in Vidarbha. Without hesitation, Gandhi moved into that land. There were no roads, no facilities. Villagers were starkly poor. One night, Kasturba fell ill. Gandhi had to move her on a bullock cart and walk for hours in the dark rainy night to reach the nearest hospital in Wardha. Once Ba was cured, Gandhi was back at the village.

Gandhi and Vivekananda had never met. But after a visit to the Belur Mutt, Gandhi confessed that his patriotism had grown manifold after reading about Vivekananda. Vivekananda had, in an electrifying speech, talked about the three qualities needed for all the social reformers. First was an intense feeling. He piercingly asked the countrymen, 'Do you feel? Do you feel that millions are starving today and millions have been starving for ages? Do you feel that ignorance has come upon this nation as a dark cloud? Does it make you restless? Does it make you sleepless? Has it entered your blood, coursing through your veins, become almost consonant with your heartbeat? Have you almost become mad with that one idea of the misery of your own people and forgotten about your name, fame and prosperity?' But intense feeling is not everything. Once you have that feeling, look for a way to alleviate the sufferings of the people. The story doesn't end there also. The most difficult part, according to Vivekananda, was to plunge into the path you have chosen and work. Then and then alone, can you be a real reformer.

Gandhi had fully internalised and lived Vivekananda's message for the reformers. On the day when the nation was celebrating independence, Gandhi was not in Delhi. He was away at Noakhali in Bengal, among the victims of the worst communal riot that had taken place.

Barack Obama, while visiting a school in 2015, was asked by a student as to what had inspired him that led to his becoming the first-ever African-American president of America. Obama said that it was Gandhi. 'He gave voice to the voiceless; gave them confidence to rise,' said Obama, repeating Czech scholar Václav Havel's famous statement about the 'power of the powerless'.

There were many in the last century who had worked for the amelioration of the sufferings of the downtrodden. Dr Bhimrao Ambedkar was one among them. Ambedkar had given India a Constitution that was like a beacon of hope to those sections. Ambedkar saw the problems of the downtrodden as social and economic. Hindus and Christians saw those as religious. But

Gandhi saw them as moral. Not coercion, nor conversion; but moral reformation should be the way, he believed. Through Harijan Sewak Sangh, he not only wanted the scheduled caste brethren to gain self-confidence but also majorly worked for reform in the thinking of the other sections of the society.

When the Indian Constitution was promulgated, Ambedkar had said that the ideals that inspired the French Revolution—liberty, equality and fraternity—had also found their reflection in it. Liberty and equality could be achieved through constitutional means. Our Constitution provides for the two ideals and also the laws to punish violators. But the third ideal, fraternity, cannot be achieved through mere constitutional mechanisms. It requires public education. For example, untouchability and caste discrimination have been declared as crimes in the Constitution; they are banished from public life. But have they gone from our hearts and minds?

In Gandhi's and Ambedkar's time, the struggle was for according equal status to the downtrodden. Programmes like temple entry and common dining were the order of the day. But today the aspirations have changed. The discourse today is no longer about those things anymore. It is about a role in decision-making and an urge for dignity, not charity. Do the downtrodden really have a role in deciding about their own destiny and the destiny of the nation? Or, they are up there just for public display? Despite reservations and affirmative action, how many of them are there today in the bureaucracy, judiciary and academics in decision-making positions? It should be the logical next step in Gandhian reform.

So much filth has been written about Gandhi and women. Gandhi lived a transparent life. He would never sleep with the doors and windows of his bedroom shut. How many of us do that? He had enormous respect for women. He declared that he would consider that day as the real day of independence when a woman in this country would roam about freely on the streets alone at midnight. Many would interpret it as a suggestion for the security of women. It is, but it is more than that.

It is about the way we look at and treat our women. Do we see it as an equal right of a woman, just like that of a man, to be seen on the streets at midnight? Or do we perceive those women as promiscuous and with loose morals? Perhaps Gandhi was indicating about the need for a perceptional reform. We talk so much about security of women. It is important. We have laws for the same. Nirbhaya law is the latest and most stringent. Yet, have the atrocities on women stopped? Can laws ensure full safety and security for women? What is of equal importance together with laws is to change the perception of the society about women.

To talk about empowerment, et cetera, is patronising today. Some are clichés like 'worship of women', et cetera. What women want today is dignity and respect. That was the reply given by Vivekananda when someone asked him about women's security. Laughing out loudly at the question, Vivekananda reminds the questioner, that women are Shakti, Durga and Bhagwati. No one needs to protect them, they can do that themselves. But everyone needs to respect them. Respect and dignity, with no riders like how they dress or how they look, is what the society needs to be taught about its outlook towards women.

'Gandhi can be killed, but not Gandhism,' declared Gandhi. Gandhism for the 21st century lies in the principles like dignity, equal participation in decision-making and respect.

Gandhi's life was a pilgrimage. He had gone on experimenting with his life, learning through those experiences and in the end, left behind a rich repository of wisdom for generations to come.

Chalte Chalte Raah Ban Gaye;
Jalte Jalte Daah Ban Gaye;
Bhakt Swayam Bhagwan Ban Gaye
(By treading the chosen path, he became the path himself; by burning in the fire, he became the flames himself; by prayer and meditation, the devotee himself became the deity.)

This famous poem of Atal Bihari Vajpayee aptly applies to Gandhi. Atalji had ended the poem by saying:

Aaj nahi vah, kintu path par
Charan chinh ankit hai,
Manu ke vamsaj pralay kaal se
Kyun shankit hai
Yadi Ramakrishna gaye, to Vivekananda sesh hai
(He is no more today, but the footsteps remain. Why should the descendants of Manu be apprehensive of the impending disasters? Ramakrishna has gone, but Vivekanandas are still there.)

Gandhi is no more; but there are Gandhians who can inspire us and lead us in creating more Gandhians through the true ideals of Gandhism.

4

The Beauty of Indic Thought

Indic thought is the most liberal that the world has ever produced. This is because it is the most democratically evolved of all. It is a product of the deep contemplation of great sages and saints, their great dialogues and discourses. A *bhadra icchha*, a benign wish had originated from that, and it was about *abhyudaya*, progress and prosperity.

> *Bhadram icchhantah rishiyah*
> *swar vidayah, tapo dikshaamupanshed agre.*
> *Tato raashtram, bala, ojasya jaatam*
> *tadasmai devaupasannmantu*

That *bhadra icchha* led to the evolution of the core principles of Indic thought several millennia ago. It explored all dimensions of human existence, and concluded that life is a celebration. 'Aananda', eternal bliss, is the ultimate objective of this. Indic Thought teaches us to celebrate life.

A few years ago, I was at a conference in China. A Chinese scholar had made a startling comment that Indians can never compete with the Chinese. I asked him to explain. 'You Indians are worshippers of poverty,' he insisted, saying that Indians worship loin-cloth-clad saintly men as heroes, whereas the Chinese civilisation had always worshipped prosperity.

It prompted me to wonder whether they have misunderstood our worldview. We are the people who always strived for 'aananda', eternal bliss.

Alexander bumps into Diogenes, a half-naked man lying on the banks of a river on his way. He asks the man, 'Who are you?' The man says that he is Diogenes. And then he asks Alexander, 'Who are you?' A little surprised and a lot annoyed, Alexander replies, 'I am Alexander the Great.' Hearing it, Diogenes laughs out aloud. 'I am seeing a man for the first time who calls himself "the Great",' he says.

They engage in a discussion. At the end, impressed by Diogenes's philosophy, Alexander promises to become his disciple. 'Do it today, or it will be too late,' warns Diogenes. Alexander hesitates, 'I have a mission to conquer the world. I shall come back after that,' he promises. 'You can never,' says Diogenes. 'Can I do something for you?' asks Alexander. 'Yes! I am enjoying my beautiful sun bath. You are coming in the way. Please move away,' shouts Diogenes.

Alexander was looking for his happiness in wars, conquest and subjugation. Diogenes, a saintly man, finds it in his freedom to lie down by the side of the river for a sun bath. Freedom, absolute and unmitigated, is the Indic way.

'God is dead; Man is free,' exclaimed Nietzsche. But we said, 'No. God is here, and hence man is free.' God is all around. He is in me. I am God, the unbound. Hence, I am free. We are a society that cherishes freedom.

Our Dharma, a view and vision of life that has evolved out of this thought, is the Dharma of happiness and celebration. '*Sarve api sukhinah santu*' is our daily morning prayer. At one level, it is purely a material prayer. It says, 'Let all be happy; let all be free from disease; let all enjoy goods in life; let all be free of sorrow'. It is about material happiness.

But the operational word in this prayer is 'sarvepi' or 'all'. We pray that everybody should be happy. In order for all to be happy, all have to also sacrifice. 'Tyaaga', sacrifice, is thus made a virtue for the greater aananda of society.

Indic Thought is very profound, and yet very humble. It doesn't ordain any final word and demand that followers believe it. We are not 'believers', we are 'seekers'. Indic Thought is man's journey, an unending exploration of the Absolute.

Since we are seekers, we have to be ever open to new ideas. We shouldn't assume that all the Indic wisdom can be available in a single gathering. Humility, the quality of accepting our inadequacy to realise the Ultimate Truth, and a constant yearning for it, is best captured in the Indic concept of 'Neti Neti'. Scholars have interpreted it in many ways: 'Neither this nor that'. But Chaturvedi Badrinath's interpretation, 'Not just this alone', best captures the Indic spirit. In our seeking, we must not forget that what we explore is not the entire truth. We must respect the other; continue to seek.

The seeker has no boundaries. He can find virtue anywhere in the world. 'Hold your own values with one hand, close to your heart. Stretch your other hand into the universe, and collect as much wisdom as you can,' exhorted Swami Vivekananda. Indic Thought doesn't discard any idea based on its origin, East or West. It accepts all noble thoughts. Any effort to restrict it in a framework will be the 'Victorianisation' of Indic Thought. It will be the death of it.

Indic Thought wants humans to evolve in inner spaces, not just in outer morals. Semitic faiths and Victorians have emphasised 'character'. This English word has two equivalent Hindi words: 'sheel' and 'charitra'. The latter is a discipline imposed from outside. Social norms, ethics, societal morals—all these form your 'charitra'. But 'sheel' is the blossoming of the inner self; it is not bound by external restrictions; it is an innate virtue.

Go to an uneducated old woman of the poorest household in a remote village in our country. Listen to her morning prayer. She might not have enough food to eat for the day, or enough clothes to wear. But her prayer will be: '*Ganga maiyya ki jai ho; gau mata ki jai ho*', 'Glory to the Ganges and the revered cow'. And it will end with '*Lok kalyaan ho*', 'Let the whole world be happy.' It was not taught to her; it is her 'sheel' speaking.

Religions have imposed so-called values externally. They wanted society to have character. One should never become 'dus-charitra', a man of bad character. But one shouldn't remain 'charitravaan', a man of external character, alone. One should become 'sheelvaan', a man of innate virtue. That is Indic Thought.

It is this virtue that might sometimes seem to go against societal mores, which is the real freedom that Indic Thought accords to the individual. Because many a time, these norms that we construct—for 'charitra'—might end up subjecting some sections of people to injustice. Victims of this are true minorities. A minority is not defined numerically; it refers to those whose voice has been taken away. Discrimination on the basis of sex, caste or race, even in the name of social character, is against Indic Thought.

Draupadi is the epitome of 'sheel'. She is in a way the first feminist of the world. A woman with five husbands, but fiercely independent, as she is not to obey any of them and only listen to her dear colleague Krishna. Draupadi was partly responsible for the epic Kurukshetra War described in Mahabharata. Yudhisthira, being Dharmaraj, was willing to settle for five villages. But Krishna turns to Draupadi, and it was she who insists that she wouldn't settle for anything less, quite rightfully, than the blood of Dushasana. It was Draupadi's 'sheel', not Yudhisthira's 'charitra' of peace and no-war that finally led to the victory of Dharma. We didn't call Draupadi an obdurate woman; instead, we call her Maha Sadhvi, an epitome of virtue.

Indic Thought is about promoting and respecting that 'sheel', irrespective of whether one is born as a man or a woman, or even a transgender person.

Such a profound and evolved way of thought has still not taken its rightful place in the world. It is still regarded as regressive and obscurantist. But as Gandhiji rightly used to say, 'If there is something bad in your society, don't blame Dharma; blame yourself, that you have failed to realise it fully.' We have to realise it. More importantly, we have to articulate it properly.

That is the challenge. I have another one to proffer: think of ways to make Indic Thought fashionable, something that a 21st century young man would like to wear on his sleeve.

5

Three Warnings of B.R. Ambedkar

Dr Babasaheb Ambedkar was the prime architect of the Indian Constitution. He put his heart and soul into it and gave to a complex and diverse country like India a comprehensive document in the form of the Constitution on 26 November 1949.

Dr Ambedkar is no doubt remembered fondly by the nation on several occasions every year; on his birth and death anniversaries and on the Republic Day, and of late, since last couple of years, on the newly conceived Constitution Day. One thing is conspicuous in all these events. Dr Ambedkar is remembered largely for his commitment to and efforts for social justice. His clarion call for fraternity, besides liberty and equality, his emphasis on social equality, besides constitutional and political equality through 'one man one vote regime' are all remembered as his greatest contributions.

They are all important contributions of Dr Ambedkar to the downtrodden of India. But he is not just that alone; he is that and much more. The very Constitution that he had strived so hard to put in place was not just about any single issue or community. It is about the entire spectrum of the private and public life of over 450 million citizens at that time, and by extension 1.25 billion citizens now. Dr Ambedkar was concerned about the plight of the downtrodden; but he was also concerned about the larger well-being of the entire nation. He saw in the Constitution a hope for the downtrodden as well as an order in the larger Indian society. He laid all his hopes of success of the Constitution on its true masters, the people of India.

Joseph Story, an eminent jurist and commentator of the Constitution and politics was to America what Nani Palkhivala was to India. Talking about the US Constitution, Joseph Story observed: 'The Constitution has been reared for immortality if the work of man may justly aspire to such a title. It may, nevertheless, perish in an hour, by the folly, or corruption, or negligence of its only keepers, the people'.

Dr Ambedkar too expressed the same apprehension about the Indian Constitution and politics. 'However good a Constitution may be, it is sure to turn out bad because those who are called to work it, happen to be a bad lot', he once said. Despite the hard work and dedication that has gone into making of the Constitution, Dr Ambedkar knew fully well that it fails to deliver if the keepers of it, the good people, lethargic and indifferent, thinking that politics as a vocation is all scum, stay away from it; and the bad and ugly in the society come to occupy the positions of power.

As Carne Ross puts it in *The Leaderless Revolution*, democracies facilitate an honourable agreement between the people—the electors, and the government—the elected. The Constitution is in reality the document of that solemn agreement between the elector and the elected. Unfortunately, at least in India, people hardly know their Constitution well. Sections of the society, whose interests the Constitution intends to protect, know a little or a lot only about those sections of the Constitution that are intended to safeguard their interests. But the larger intent and import of the Constitution is hardly known to the people.

On 26 November, speaking on the occasion of the Constitution Day, President Ram Nath Kovind highlighted precisely the same thing. 'It is a paradox that our citizens, in whose name the Constitution was adopted, are sometimes not sufficiently informed about what the Constitution means for us. Let the 70th year of its adoption be dedicated to enhancing awareness about the Constitution', he said in his address to the nation.

In fact, although the final draft of the Constitution was passed by the Constituent Assembly on 26 November 1949, and subsequently the same was adopted as the Constitution of India on 26 January 1950, no special effort was ever made in all these years to inform and educate the people about it. It was only in 2015, sixty-five years after its adoption, that Prime Minister Modi thought of celebrating the Constitution Day annually with the objective of letting its keepers, the people, know about it well.

Lack of awareness about the Constitution among the larger masses allowed for the intermediate forces, some of whom are the products of that very Constitution itself, to subvert its spirit and thus leading to the violation of that solemn agreement between the voter and the voted. Dr Ambedkar had warned about this possibility in his last address to the Constituent Assembly one day before its passing, on 25 November 1949.

In that speech, famously known as 'Three Warnings', Dr Ambedkar raised the spectre of India losing its independence once again if the Constitution was not adhered to in letter and spirit:

> On 26th January, 1950, India will be an independent country. What would happen to her independence? Will she maintain

her independence or will she lose it again? This is the first thought that comes to my mind. It is not that India was never an independent country. The point is that she once lost the independence she had. Will she lose it a second time? It is this thought which makes me most anxious for the future. What perturbs me greatly is the fact that not only India has once before lost her independence, but she lost it by the infidelity and treachery of some of her own people.

The constitutional governance faces challenges from its own limbs like the judiciary, bureaucracy and the political establishment internally. Externally too, today, it faces a serious challenge from certain group interests championed by forces that are not accountable, nor representative of the masses.

Judiciary is an important branch of our Constitution. In a way, the only branch that still keeps the hopes of justice of large sections of the masses alive. But of late, the surviving institution of people's trust too seems to be passing through a phase that poses a challenge to the genuine upholding of the interests of the people.

One important case in the recent times attracts our attention to this. Justice delayed or justice hurried, both lead to justice denied. In the first instance is the Ram Janmabhoomi case, a matter pending before the Supreme Court for the last six years. The simple question referred to them was whether the order of the Allahabad High Court trifurcating the main temple compound where once a temple, followed by a mosque had stood and currently a make-shift temple of Ram Lalla stands, is valid or not.

It took five years for the Supreme Court to open the matter in the middle of 2017, only to discuss the issue of translating all the relevant documents—some 14,000 pages, which were in

Hindi, Urdu and other languages, into English. Who will take responsibility for translation? Finally, the UP Government came forward to do that.

Then the Court suddenly found the issue of relevance and importance of mosque to Islam as a major question for adjudication. That the said question, may be important in some other context, was completely extraneous to the present case, didn't find favour with the learned judges. That issue too was finally settled and the previous Chief Justice had announced that the expeditious hearing of the main case would begin on 29 October 2018. In the first week of October, the Supreme Court got a new Chief Justice. When the matter came up before the bench headed by the new Chief Justice, it took just three minutes for him to declare that the Ram Janmabhoomi matter was not a 'priority' to the Court. He pushed the matter to a later date in January 2019.

It should go to their credit that the parties involved, both the protagonists of the temple and their adversaries, have thus far laid their hopes on the Supreme Court. But now, the unintended consequence of the Supreme Court's declaration was that they had to turn it into a 'priority'. That is why we see enhanced activity in the country, including massive mobilisations in favour of the temple. Such instances showcase the challenge to the Constitution from judicial activism leading thereby to the violation of the solemn agreement.

The other challenge comes from the second organ of our constitutional government, the bureaucracy. Speaking at an event, former President Dr Pranab Mukherjee called the bureaucracy as the biggest impediment to development. 'Bureaucracy is the biggest hurdle of our development and we must rectify it', he said. Not that individual bureaucrats are bad. But bureaucracy as a system and an institution has the potential of derailing the efforts of the political establishment and denying justice to the people.

Then comes the role of the political parties. Dr Ambedkar, in his last address to the Constituent Assembly, had warned, 'If the parties place creed above country, our independence will be put in a jeopardy a second time and probably be lost forever'. Today, we see a situation where the national parties are increasingly becoming marginalised and a large number of regional and other group-based parties are emerging with strong constituencies of their own.

It will be unwise to dismiss the rise of these identity-based groups and parties. It is a global phenomenon today. In a scintillating work titled *Political Tribes*, well-known author Amy Chua writes: 'We tend to view the world in terms of territorial nation-states engaged in great ideological battles—Capitalism versus Communism, Democracy versus Authoritarianism, the 'Free World' versus the 'Axis of Evil'. Blinded by our own ideological prisms, we have repeatedly ignored more primal group identities, which for billions are the most powerful and meaningful, and which drive political upheaval all over the world'. The Constitution has been facing this acute challenge from identity groups that don a political avatar.

The third challenge comes from causes that largely the Teflon-coated Liberals champion. They pick up certain myopic concepts, and, using the systemic loopholes, attempt to subvert the very spirit of the Constitution itself. In that, they get help from their fellow ideological travellers in various important institutions. Their agendas are narrow and in most cases lofty, but largely unconnected with the reality of the masses. They co-opt political actors or sometimes themselves become one, but are not really accountable to any. These groups include certain NGO activists too. Their influence is enormous these days because it is fashionable to associate with the causes they champion, despite the fact that they hardly represent any significant section of the population.

'A growing number of political actors, who are neither politicians nor conventional political parties, nor accountable to anyone but themselves, are wielding enormous influence over policy-making these days', rues Carne Ross, former British diplomat in his book *The Leaderless Revolution*.

One latest example of the influence these groups enjoy is the Sabarimala temple issue. A harmless tradition at a temple of Lord Ayyappa in Kerala was challenged as spurious, on the ground that it is against gender equality. Those who challenged it using certain Constitutional provisions pertaining to the Fundamental Rights didn't include a single devotee. On the contrary, the petitioners claimed that they were non-believers and had nothing to do with the given temple or its traditions. That teaching gender equality to a matriarchal society like Kerala, where women lead the social life in all spheres, including religion, is like carrying coal to Newcastle, or that not a single woman devotee came forward to demand entry into the temple couldn't stop the Supreme Court in deciding to throw open the doors to women in the age group of 10 and 50.

It has resulted in a situation where the State Government led by God-less Marxists in Kerala forcing a break in the tradition by compelling women to enter the temple and the tens of thousands of religious women coming out on to the streets in all Kerala towns and villages demanding that the order be withdrawn. Another classic example of what the people want their rulers to do and what the middlemen want to impose on them. While jealously safeguarding the individual rights, we tend to forget that people also enjoy certain 'group rights' and they too need safeguarding. In fact, the Indian Constitution recognises this through several of its articles, including articles 25 to 30 that cover a gamut of rights of the religious groups.

Democracy is described as a government 'Of the people, By the people and For the people'. It no doubt continues to be a government 'of' and 'by' the people. But it increasingly ceases to be 'for' the people. Instead, it is becoming a prisoner in the hands of group and narrow political interests. Dr Ambedkar and Joseph Story were both referring to this danger.

6

Cultivating Constitutional Morality

Seventy years ago, on this day, the Indian Constitution was finally signed and sealed by the Constituent Assembly. It was the first ever democratic Constitution that India had adopted. In the past, we used to have smritis that contained rules for social order. Smritis were rendered by men of wisdom like Narada, Yajnavalkya and Manu. They were not binding on society. Yet, largely, contemporary societies had accepted them as guides for social behaviour. Some scholars describe the Indian Constitution as Ambedkar Smriti. The role that Dr Ambedkar had played in drafting this Constitution was phenomenal. It was to draw from many sources, including the Government of India Act, 1935 and constitutions of various Western countries, yet it had to be quintessentially Indian. In the end, that was what we got on 26 November 1949, courtesy the efforts of Ambedkar and his team.

Ambedkar, the architect of our Constitution, had delivered a brilliant speech one day before, on 25 November, highlighting threats to the Constitution. That speech became famous as 'Ambedkar's Three Warnings'. The first warning he gave was about strict adherence to constitutional methods in 'achieving our social and economic objectives'. Means are as important as the ends, Gandhiji, whose portrait used to be placed above the podium of the chairman of the Constituent Assembly, used to insist. Ambedkar's second warning was about hero worship. 'Bhakti in religion may be a road to the salvation of the soul. But in politics, hero worship is a sure road to degeneration and to eventual dictatorship,' he warned. Quoting Irish patriot Daniel O'Connel, who said, 'no man can be grateful at the cost of his honour; no woman can be grateful at the cost of her chastity; and no nation can be grateful at the cost of its liberty,' Ambedkar had said that caution was far more necessary for India than any other country. His third warning was that we shouldn't be content with mere political democracy and strive to achieve social democracy as well. 'Political democracy cannot last unless there lies at the base of it, social democracy,' he cautioned.

Ambedkar's warnings were far-reaching. But equally important, although less talked about, was the speech of the chairman of the Constituent Assembly and the first President of India, Dr Rajendra Prasad. He delivered the last address to the Assembly before the Constitution was signed on 26 November 1949. For the first time, universal adult franchise was introduced despite reservations from some. Rajendra Prasad had defended it in his address by saying:

> I am a man of the village and my roots are still there. I, therefore, know the village people who will constitute the bulk of this vast electorate. In my opinion, our people possess intelligence and common sense. They also have a culture which the sophisticated people of today may not appreciate, but which is solid. They are not literate and do not possess the mechanical skill of reading and writing. But I have no doubt in my mind that they are able to take measure of their own interest and also of the interests of the country at large if things are explained to them.

Interestingly, one of the major regrets of Rajendra Prasad was that the Constitution couldn't lay down some qualifications for the members of the legislature. 'It is anomalous that we should insist upon high qualifications for those who administer or help in administering the law but none for those who made it except that they are elected,' he bemoaned.

Rajendra Prasad's words are significant. Although the Constitution has created three pillars of governance—legislature, administration and judiciary—the real protectors of the Constitution are those who sit in the legislatures. It is the Parliament, the elected body of the people's representatives, which is the heart of our Constitution. The Parliament, as Prime Minister Modi put it, is like a temple. Its sacredness needs to be upheld always. The death knell of the Constitution is in the degeneration of the Parliament.

It is the case not just with India, but with all democracies. Parliamentary democracies arose as an answer to the selfish and untalented monarchs and dictators in the last two centuries. It is through the parliaments that charismatic leaders acquire power and give dynamism and direction to countries. And therein lies the protection of the Constitution too. In other words, the welfare and well-being of the country depends on the quality of our parliamentarians. The parliamentarians too face a challenge that Max Weber, the eminent political philosopher, had highlighted very rightly. Charismatic leaders and powerful parties make the role of the parliamentarians rather constrained. They are mostly reduced to 'well-disciplined lobby fodder', according to Weber.

That was why Rajendra Prasad had done some plain-speaking in his final address. 'If the people who are elected are capable and men of character and integrity, they would be able to make the best even of a defective Constitution. If they are lacking in these, the Constitution cannot help the country. After all, a Constitution, like a machine, is a lifeless thing. It acquires life because of the men who control it and operate it, and India needs today nothing more than a set of honest men who will have the interest of the country before them. It requires men of strong character, men of vision, men who will not sacrifice the interests of the country at large for the sake of smaller groups and areas and who will rise over the prejudices which are born of these differences. We can only hope that the country will throw up such men in abundance,' he said.

When the Constitution turns seventy, the country is blessed with a leadership that truly represents such men. If the mission of the Constitution were to be described in one word, it is justice. The upholders of the Constitution should try to render justice to the last man on the street. 'Man is born free, but everywhere he is in chains,' lamented Rousseau. Ambedkar had seen these chains as social and economic. For Gandhi and Vinoba Bhave, they were moral. The Constitution's mandate was to remove those chains so that people of this country enjoy justice—social, economic and moral.

Ambedkar had said that the ideals that inspired the French Revolution—liberty, equality and fraternity—were the ones that formed the core of the Indian Constitution too. Liberty and equality are achievable through constitutional means, whereas for achieving fraternity, laws are not sufficient. A constant endeavour to render justice to all sections of the society can only engender fraternity. As long as a section of the people feels discriminated against, the sense of brotherhood can't be achieved. Not just the state, but society too needs to shoulder responsibility for it.

The spirit of the Constitution needs to be guarded not only by parliamentarians but also by the people with utmost sacredness. That is called constitutional morality.

As Ambedkar had put it, 'Constitutional morality is not a natural sentiment. It needs to be cultivated.' Let the nation dedicate itself to the task of cultivating that.

7

Samajik Samrasta (Social Harmony)
Shri Guruji M.S. Golwalkar

Three famous ideals that inspired the French Revolution i.e., Liberty, Equality and Fraternity have subsequently found place in almost all the democratic constitutions of the world including ours. Liberty and Equality are the ideals that can be achieved through constitutional means. But for achieving Fraternity we need something more than constitutional means.

That is why Dr B.R. Ambedkar, the architect of our Constitution had attached greater significance to this ideal of Fraternity.

'What does Fraternity mean?' he questioned, and went on to explain that 'Fraternity means a sense of common brotherhood of all Indians—of Indians being one people. It is this principle that gives unity and solidarity to social life.' Fraternity is not just an institutional reality like Liberty and Equality. It has an emotional quotient—a feeling of brotherhood and oneness. The national mind has to be trained through Samskaras to acquire this feeling.

Samata, Samaanta and Samarasata: these three words are quite common in our public parlance. Samata is equality in thoughts; Samaanta is equality in law; but Samarasata is equality of emotions and feelings. For achieving Samarasata—social harmony to put it simply—fraternity is the basic requirement.

Bharat from time immemorial has championed the idea of the quintessential oneness of the universe. World's ancient-most literature—the Vedas—categorically reject the idea of inequality and insist upon oneness at the emotional level and equality at the mundane level.

Ajyesthaaso Akanisthaasa Yete
Sam Bhraataro Vaavrudhuh Soubhagaya
　　　　　　　　　　　Rigveda, Mandala-5, Sukta-60, Mantra-5

'No one is superior or inferior; all are brothers; all should strive for the interest of all and collective progress'.

Samaani va Aakootihi Samaanaa Hridayaanivah
Samaanamastu vo Mano Yathaa Vah Susahaasati
　　　　　　　　　　　Rigveda, Mandala-10, Sukta-191, Mantra-4

'Let there be oneness in your resolutions, hearts and minds; let the determination to live with mutual cooperation be firm in you all'.

It is worthwhile to mention here that it was much later that the world had come up with the ideals of French Revolution or for that matter the first Article of the Universal Declaration of Human Rights (1948) that exhorts:

All human beings are born free and equal in dignity and rights. They are endowed with reason and conscience and should act towards one another in a spirit of brotherhood.

However, in its long journey of thousands of years that very nation which had offered such lofty ideals to the mankind landed itself in a state of decay and disintegration. Several social evils and weaknesses have crept into the body politic of this ancient nation.

Over the years, its diversity became its disunity; institutions came to represent its decay; and social evils like untouchability and caste discrimination became rampant.

There was never a scriptural sanction to social evils like untouchability and caste discrimination. In fact, the history of the progress of our nation is also the history of countless social reformers, saints and savants who struggled against these social evils thus ensuring unity and longevity of our nation.

Adishankara's Advaita to Gandhiji's Ram Rajya and Ambedkar's social movement; Ramanuja's Visisthaadvaita to RSS's Hindu Rashtra—countless reform movements have swept across this vast nation over the ages with the singular objective of preserving the unity and harmony. Buddha, Mahaveera, Basaveshwara, Kanakadasa, Ramakrishna, Vivekananda, Narayana Guru, Dayananda Saraswati, Tilak, Gandhi, Ambedkar, Savarkar, Jyotiba Phule—endless is the list of greatmen who have sacrificed their lives in the pursuit of achieving the lofty ideal of social harmony.

The RSS is the continuation of that great tradition set in motion by the above-mentioned savants and social reformers. The founder of the RSS, Dr Hedgewar was anguished by the utter disunity in the Hindu society and was inspired by the efforts of great social reformers. While starting the RSS, he had only one vision—of a nation rising like one man symbolising all that is good in its ancient wisdom and discarding everything that is alien to its core thought of universal oneness. He did not preach much; but the institution of the RSS that he had created spoke volumes through its activity.

In 1934, when Gandhiji visited a 1500-strong Swayamsevaks camp at Wardha in Vidarbha, he was pleasantly surprised to find that the Swayamsevaks were not even aware of the castes of one another, not to speak of any idea of untouchability. Later, he invited Dr Hedgewar to his Ashram and enquired about the RSS's activities. The visit had left such a deep impression on Gandhiji's mind that he referred to it full thirteen years later. In his address to the workers of Sangh in Bhangi Colony at Delhi on 16 September 1947, he said, 'I visited the RSS camp years ago, when the founder Shri Hedgewar was alive. I was very much impressed by your discipline, the complete absence of untouchability and the rigorous simplicity. Since then, the Sangh has grown. I am convinced that any organisation which is inspired by the high ideal of service and self-sacrifice is bound to grow in strength.'

When Dr Babasaheb Ambedkar visited Sangh Shiksha Varga in Pune in 1939, he was also surprised to find the Swayamsevaks moving about in absolute equality. When Dr Ambedkar asked Dr Hedgewar whether there were any untouchables in the camp, the latter replied that there were neither touchables nor untouchables, but only Hindus. Recording his appreciation Dr Ambedkar said, 'I am surprised to find the Swayamsevaks moving about in absolute equality and brotherhood without even caring to know the caste of the others.'

Shri M.S. Golwalkar alias Guruji, who became the Sarsanghachalak of the RSS in 1940, was originally molded in the tradition of those great saints and sages. 'While the present day West has not been able to go beyond the motto of the 'greatest good of the greatest number', we have never tolerated the idea of a single human being, nay, even a single living organism living in misery. 'Total good of all beings' has always been our glorious ideal', exhorted Shri Guruji. He worked relentlessly for 33 years with that as the mission and left an inerasable imprint on our national life.

It was under the stewardship of Shri Guruji that the Sangh work had expanded to include a large number of activities for the welfare of tribals and backward classes. Many organisations and activists were working among these sections striving for their upliftment. However, Shri Guruji insisted that the reform is needed not just in the backwards and tribals alone, but in the so-called Savarnas as well.

Dr Ambedkar, fully endorsing the views of Shri Guruji, had said that it is not enough if the activity of Dalit Uddhar is limited to the Dalits alone; it should come from within the so-called Savarna society also.

In a sense, Shri Guruji made the ideal of Dalit Uddhar not a voluntary activity, but a natural and fundamental duty of the entire society. 'It is our utmost important duty to serve the brothers who are neglected and we have to improve their life in various fields. We have to prepare plans for this,' he told the Hindu society.

As mentioned above, Samarasata is emotional oneness. In order for this to be achieved we need to remove the mental blocks in various sections of our society. Our society is divided into various castes and sub-castes. Some castes are considered high and some others low. There is a misguided hierarchical caste structure still in vogue. It is creating great fissures in our society.

Several reformers have tried through different means to achieve harmony. Gandhiji gave the name Harijan to a group of so-called lower castes and tried to impress upon the rest of the society that they were the men of Hari. Dr Ambedkar wrote *Annihilation of Caste*. Socialists have tried to create 'caste-less society' through organisations like 'Jaati-Paati Todak Mandal'. Each had their own experiences.

Shri Guruji adopted a totally different approach. Instead of working on the differences in our society he emphasised on the fundamental unity of our nation. A major landmark in this direction was the establishment of the Vishwa Hindu Parishad (VHP) in 1964. Awakening the age-old wisdom of fundamental oneness of the universe and ideal of universal love in the society is the best way to achieve Samarasata, according to Shri Guruji. He chose the VHP as the vehicle for achieving this transformation in the society.

The 1969 conclave of the VHP in Udupi was a major turning point in the history of the Hindu society in this regard. For the first time in recent history, a large number of saints and savants from almost all traditions and denominations of the Hindu society had come together under one umbrella of the VHP. Shri Guruji had personally invited each one of them and supervised the whole conclave.

A historic resolution was unanimously passed by all the assembled Mahatmas that read:

> It is now up to us to go to those neglected brethren of our society and strive our utmost to better their living conditions. We will have to work out plans by which their primary material needs and comforts could be fulfilled. We will have to open schools, hostels and training programmes to equip them to benefit from these schemes. Alongside this material amelioration, love and pride in Hindu Dharma and the spirit of identity with the entire Hindu society have to be rekindled in their minds through the channels of devotion to God. For that, we have to give up notions of high and low and mingle with those brethren in a

spirit of equality. We should freely mingle with them, eat with them and sing the songs of devotion with them.

A momentous occasion in the Hindu history came when Swami Pujya Vishweswar Teerthaji of Pejawar Mutt gave a clarion call from that dais: '*Hindavah Sodaraah Sarve*' (All Hindus are brothers and sisters) and '*Na Hinduh Patito Bhavet*' (A Hindu can never be fallen). He also gave a new mantra to the Hindu society: '*Mama Deeksha Hindu Raksha-Mama Mantrah Samanata*' (Protecting Hindu society is my mission and equality is my Mantra).

The RSS has tread the path set by the revered saints and covered a large space in achieving social harmony. There cannot be any revolutionary solutions to the disharmony that we witness in our society. Caste system, which has become the central reason for disharmony today, needs to be reformed. 'Old order passeth yielding place to new lest one good custom corrupt the world,' said Alfred Tennyson in The *Passing of Arthur*. But this change can be achieved only through sustained and positive efforts and a deep commitment to the fundamental cultural unity of our society.

Today, if the RSS stands like a beacon of that unity in the otherwise strife-torn and disharmonious Hindu society, it is because of the stewardship of great social reformers like Dr Hedgewar and Shri Guruji.

8

Deendayal Upadhyaya
The Swayamsewak

Syama Prasad Mookerjee walked out of Jawaharlal Nehru's cabinet due to ideological differences and started the Bharatiya Jana Sangh (BJS) in 1950. When he approached the RSS for support, the leadership decided to second some of its best pracharaks, including Deendayal Upadhyaya, Atal Bihari Vajpayee, Lal Krishna Advani, Sundar Singh Bhandari and Nanaji Deshmukh. Upadhyaya, who would have turned 103 today, became the general secretary of the BJS in the party's very first session in December 1951 and worked in that capacity for 16 years.

The emergence of BJS was a historic development. The BJS was not just another political outfit but a party with a distinct philosophy and programme. The Congress was the dominant party at that time. The Hindu Maha Sabha, Ram Rajya Parishad and Swatantra Party were no match to the ruling establishment. The communists and socialists too lacked a national appeal and charismatic leadership. The BJS was established to offer a quintessentially Indian alternative to Nehru's politics and political philosophy.

For Upadhyaya, politics wasn't just for capturing power. He would insist on practising value-based and principled politics. The central thrust of his politics was national interest. He was, in fact, a reluctant politician. His mentor, M.S. Golwalkar of the RSS, once said, 'Deendayalji was the most reluctant politician, and had many times expressed his distress at the kind of work he has been entrusted with. He would rather prefer to go back to his previous work as a sangh pracharak. I told him that I could see nobody else who would do the work as well as he could. It needed an unshakable faith and complete dedication for a man to remain in this mess and yet be untouched by it.'

That parties could so easily and uninhibitedly form alliances without any commitment to principles and programmes came as a rude awakening to Upadhyaya. The changing contours of India's political landscape were unacceptable to this idealist. He once said:

> Different parties have different viewpoints. People don't take them into account. Out of goodwill, they sometimes feel that certain political parties should get together. But there are certain fundamental issues that justify separate existence of the parties. Goodwill alone is not enough. That is why we have decided that we won't live in any imaginary world and enter into an alliance whose success is doubtful. It would be good to work together on issues where a consensus is possible; otherwise we should operate from our respective platforms.

The general elections in 1967 saw the Congress decline in a number of states. Upadhyaya was forced to abandon idealism for pragmatism and realpolitik as the possibility of forming non-Congress coalition governments emerged in many states.

The Samyukt Vidhayak Dal (SVD) experiment—a non-Congress alliance of 15 parties—provided an opportunity for the BJS to become a part of the ruling establishment in several states. But it also raised the hackles of many party workers who saw the arrangement as a compromise with party ideology and beliefs. 'Let not the Jana Sangh delude itself that by cohabiting with communists, we will be able to change them. *Kharbooja chakkoo par gire, ya chakkoo kharbooja par; katega to kharbooja hi*—whether the melon falls on the knife or the knife falls on the melon, it is the melon that gets cut,' argued a party leader.

Upadhyaya had to use a combination of wisdom and realpolitik to convince the cadres about the efficacy of the SVD experiment. 'It is an irony of the country's political situation that while untouchability in the social field is considered to be evil, it is sometimes extolled as a virtue in the political field. If a party does not wish to practise untouchability towards its rival in the political establishment, it is supposed to be doing something wrong. We, in the Jana Sangh, certainly do not agree with the communist strategy, tactics and political culture. But that does not justify an attitude of untouchability towards them. If they are willing to work with us on the basis of issues, or as part of a government committed to an agreed programme, I see nothing wrong in it. The SVD governments are a step towards ending political untouchability. The spirit of accommodation shown by all parties, despite their sharp differences, is a good omen for democracy,' he argued.

Upadhyaya became president of the BJS at the party conclave in Kozhikode in December 1967. In the RSS scheme of things, pracharaks are expected only to work as the organisational backbone, never to come to the forefront. However, in the case of

Upadhyaya, an exception had to be made because of the peculiar situation that developed in the party at that juncture. Several years later, Golwalkar would throw some light on the thinking of the RSS leadership at that time. 'He [Deendayal Upadhyaya] really never wanted this high honour, nor did I wish to burden him with it. But circumstances so contrived that I had to ask him to accept the president post. He obeyed like a true swayamsevak, that he was,' said Golwalkar.

But this arrangement was short-lived. Two months after becoming the president, on 11 February 1968, Upadhyaya's body was found by the side of the railway track near Mughal Sarai station in Uttar Pradesh. He was just 52. He was the second top Jana Sangh leader to die under mysterious circumstances—the first being the founder, Syama Prasad Mookerjee, who also died mysteriously on 23 June 1953. Mookerjee too was 52 at the time of his demise.

9

Betrayal of the Mahatama

On the evening of 29 January 1948, Mohandas Gandhi told his grand-niece, Manu: 'If an explosion took place ... or someone shot at me and I received his bullet on my bare chest, without a sigh and with Rama's name on my lips, only then you should say that I was a true mahatma.' Twenty-four hours later, he stood face-to-face with a young man called Nathuram Godse.

Gandhi was late for the sermon that evening. Sardar Patel had come to discuss some issues. This became a routine during Gandhi's stay at the Birla House. Jawaharlal Nehru too used to visit him almost every evening. Although Gandhi relinquished his primary membership of the Indian National Congress some fourteen years earlier, he would always be consulted on important issues.

Gandhi was rushing towards the garden, supported by Manu and Abha, the two grandnieces whom he used to call his 'walking sticks'. Godse folded his hands and said namaste. Gandhi stopped. Suddenly, Manu was pushed to the ground. Nathuram pumped three bullets into Gandhi's bare chest and stomach. 'Hey Ra ... ma! Hey Ra ...'—this is what Manu claimed to have heard in a feeble voice. A Sikh gentleman following Gandhi too confirmed that the words of prayer came out from his lips. Gandhi was dead, his mahatma-hood having been established.

Gandhi's physical elimination was a result of the pent-up anger and frustration of a few misguided youths over what they perceived as his policy of Muslim appeasement. The ultimate provocation for them was his fast that January that had forced the Nehru cabinet to release funds to the newly-formed state of Pakistan. Those funds were withheld out of the suspicion that Pakistan would misuse them against India.

There were many who had disagreements with Gandhi, Subhas Chandra Bose and V.D. Savarkar among them. Even Nehru had serious difference of opinion with Gandhi. But to kill him needed not just difference of opinion, but a certain type of hatred borne of extreme frustration. 'A most severe austerity of life, ceaseless work and lofty character made Gandhiji formidable and irresistible,' admits Godse in his final testimony before the court. Gandhi was no doubt formidable and irresistible. Nehru once said of him: 'The essence of his teaching was fearlessness and truth and action allied to these. The voice was somehow different from others. It was quiet and low, and yet it could be heard above the shouting of the multitude; it was soft and gentle, and yet there seemed to be steel hidden away somewhere in it. Behind the language of peace and friendship, there was power and the quivering shadow of action and a determination not to submit to a wrong.'

Gandhi had a premonition about his impending death. Madanlal Pahwa attempted a bomb attack on 20 January 1948 at the Birla House. Between that day and the fateful day, Gandhi had talked about his death dozens of times. But he would steadfastly refuse security. For him, that would have been akin to violating ahimsa. People called him 'Bapu'—a father-figure. He had immense trust in the people, unlike today's leaders.

He was betrayed by those who called him Bapu and then eliminated physically, a heinous crime. Others too, who also called him Bapu and Mahatma, betrayed his principles.

On the fateful morning, Gandhi handed over the final draft of his future plan for the Indian National Congress, which he had dictated to Mirabehn a day before, to his aide Pyarelal. '... the Congress in its present shape and form, i.e., as a propaganda vehicle and parliamentary machine, has outlived its use', he declared, adding 'For these and other similar reasons, the AICC resolves to disband the existing Congress organisation and flower into a Lok Sevak Sangh.'

In fact, Gandhi had called for a meeting at Sewagram in February to discuss the plan. The meeting did take place, minus Gandhi. Nehru categorically rejected Gandhi's plan. 'Congress has now to govern. So it will have to function in a new way, staying within politics', he insisted. The lure of power overtook the ideals of service. Thus came the other betrayal.

But that was not to be the end. 'I am not going to keep quiet even after I die', Gandhi had once declared. His lifetime of work had a 'constructive' component, besides the political. Led by Gandhians like Vinoba Bhave, the constructive work had gone on. Gandhi insisted that it be 'kept out of unhealthy competition with political parties and communal bodies'. Bhave had never met Nehru while Gandhi was alive. In the first meeting at Sewagram after Gandhi's demise, he tells Nehru that he wouldn't want anything from the government; rather he would want to help Nehru if possible. Gandhians continue to strive for the goal of attaining 'social, moral and economic independence in terms of its seven hundred thousand villages' by remaining below the radar, unlike present-day NGOs that meddle in politics.

Gandhian ideas continue to influence societies in many parts of the country and the world.

'Gandhi bequeathed an example of constant striving, a set of social values, and a method of resistance, one not easily applied to an India ruled by Indians', laments Pulitzer-winning author Joseph Lelyveld in his book *Great Soul: Mahatma Gandhi and His Struggle with India*.

10

A Need for Vigilance

The Emergency wouldn't really have mattered to a ten-year-old boy like me in 1975, but for my father's arrest under the Maintenance of Internal Security Act (MISA) in the early hours of 26 June. He was a senior Jana Sangh leader in Andhra Pradesh and, hence, spent the next twenty-one months in jail. I vividly remember those days, when I used to visit him every fortnight in my mother's company. I would generally find him in good spirits. There were several other MISA detainees from his own party, as well as others in jail with him, besides those groups that would join at regular intervals under the Defence of India Rules (DIR). I used to hear from my mother that he was all right because, as a MISA detenu, he enjoyed certain facilities in jail.

While life inside jail was probably not so harsh, especially for the senior detainees arrested under MISA, life outside was just the opposite. I often heard my mother saying that life was probably more difficult for her outside than for my father inside. This had nothing to do with economic hardship. The real problem was fear. The Emergency had instilled so much fear in the country that your own kith and kin would desert you. If they didn't, the police would ensure they did, by harassing friends and relatives of detainees. I remember my family facing acute isolation, my relatives being troubled unnecessarily by the police, and friends shying away. Except for the occasional visits by RSS leaders operating underground, we didn't have much social interaction during those fateful two years.

This fear was the key to the Emergency. Independent India had never witnessed the like of that fear in the preceding twenty-five years. Whatever success stories were written about the Emergency, like the punctuality of trains or attendance in offices, were all due to this fear.

Today, when we talk about the possibility of the return of that dark era, we must not forget that while Indira Gandhi could silence the opposition by putting them behind bars, she could carry on with draconian laws for a full twenty-two months by instilling fear in the nation. She had turned the entire country into a prison of fear. There were few who didn't succumb to the fear tactic. L.K. Advani's famous quip, 'When asked to bend, they crawled', aptly sums up the mood of the nation during Emergency. The only section that stood up against the dictatorship of Indira Gandhi was the RSS cadre.

The Emergency may never return. Those who fought against this fascist action in 1975–77 are the rulers today, and their commitment to protecting democratic institutions is absolute. Democratic institutions like the media, judiciary and civic organisations are much stronger today than they were four decades ago. The democratisation of technology and information is another guarantee against any such misadventure by future rulers. Indira Gandhi could succeed in an environment of controlled media. But today, that is next to impossible. The forces that fought against the Emergency, such as the RSS, used alternate means of communication in those days. Today, it is much easier, due to the omnipresence of social media. To quote Thomas L. Friedman, 'everyone is connected and no one is in control'.

However, fear can return. For, the tools to create this fear and terror can be derived from the Constitution itself. That is what Indira Gandhi did. She manipulated the provisions of the Constitution to suit her whims and, once in control, she took to silencing the safeguards built in the Constitution too. That's how the infamous 42nd Amendment came into being.

Democracies can be illiberal while remaining democracies, argues Fareed Zakaria in his book *The Future of Freedom: Illiberal Democracy at Home and Abroad*. 'Across the globe, democratically elected regimes, through referenda, are routinely ignoring constitutional limits on their power and depriving their citizens of basic rights. This disturbing phenomenon—visible from Peru to the Palestinian territories, from Ghana to Venezuela—could be called illiberal democracy,' he avers.

While the Emergency may not return in the same form and content, we need to guard against these illiberal tendencies. Our freedom was hard-earned. Our Constitution is a document that came out of the churning of enlightened minds in the late-1940s. Eminent jurist Nani Palkhivala used to say, 'The Constitution was meant to impart such a momentum to the living spirit of the rule of law that democracy and civil liberty may survive in India beyond our own times and in the days when our place will know us no more.'

Democracy, of Herodotus's time, meant just the rule of the people. What we practise today as democracy is the rule of the majority. We have to guard against the tendencies of illiberalism in our democracy. For that, we need leaders who have absolute faith in the three cardinal principles that guided the French Revolution—liberty, equality and fraternity. 'Liberal constitutionalism', to borrow a phrase from Zakaria again, should be the order of the day. A cursory look at our political spectrum highlights the fact that the BJP is the only party with internal democracy, while most others are either family-run or feudal.

Prime Minister Narendra Modi's actions thus far clearly indicate his commitment to the liberal values of our democratic polity. His connect with the masses through programmes like *Mann ki Baat*, his respect for Parliament, his push for 'empowered federalism' and, most importantly, his total integration with social media—the torchbearer of liberal democratic principles—show that, under him, India's democracy and liberal constitutional values will be safely upheld. However, as the saying goes, 'eternal vigilance is the price to pay for freedom'.

CONFRONTING HISTORY

'Progress, far from consisting in change, depends on retentiveness. When change is absolute there remains no being to improve and no direction is set for possible improvement: and when experience is not retained, as among savages, infancy is perpetual. Those who cannot remember the past are condemned to repeat it.'

—George Santayana

11

Correcting a Historic Blunder

5 August 2019 will go down in the Constitutional history of India as a glorious day. A historic blunder committed about seventy years ago, on 17 October 1949 during the course of the Constituent Assembly debates has finally been set right. Article 370, which entered the draft Constitution seventy years ago as Article 306A, has finally been abrogated.

Nobody should complain because the abrogation of this discriminatory article has always been a running theme for the BJP and Jana Sangh. Nobody should have entertained any doubt that Prime Minister Narendra Modi, a leader possessing grit and determination, who was instrumental in hoisting the Indian Tricolour at Lal Chowk on 26 January 1992, would have spared this illogical entity in our Constitution when the appropriate moment came.

Article 370, which became history on 5 August 2019, has a notorious history. It was introduced into the draft constitution by N. Gopalaswami Ayyangar as Article 306A. Through this provision, Ayyangar had proposed that 'Kashmir state' would have special powers to be excluded from the purview of the laws that the Parliament of India would make and also would have the power to make its own laws.

'Why this discrimination?', asked Maulana Hasrat Mohani, the member from United Provinces. Ayyangar gave an unconvincing reply that there existed special circumstances in the state and hence the special provisions. He was challenged by members like Mohani who asked why different accessions were being treated differently. Ayyangar's logic was bizarre. The Instrument of Accession's relevance was limited to joining the Dominion, he argued, adding that what mattered for the Indian Republic that was going to take shape on 26 January 1950, was the decisions in the Constituent Assembly. He was no doubt clever in making this distinction between the Dominion and the Republic, but not logical.

Some five months before Ayyangar's introduction of Article 306A, on 27 May 1949, another important discussion took place on the question of nominating members to the Constituent Assembly from Jammu and Kashmir (J&K). The rules said that out of the four nominations, two may be made by the ruler and two from the provincial legislature that was in existence before the accession. The rule was scrupulously followed in the case of all the princely states, whereas in the case of J&K, Jawaharlal Nehru insisted that the Jammu Kashmir Praja Sabha, the state legislature under Maharaja Hari Singh, shouldn't be authorised to nominate the members. The Praja Sabha elections in 1946 were a fraud, insisted Nehru, and hence, he wanted the Maharaja to nominate all the four members through consultations with National Conference leader Sheikh Abdullah.

It must be noted that Sheikh Abdullah's party had boycotted the 1946 Praja Sabha elections, refusing to accept Maharaja's authority. While the rest of the country was fighting the British with Quit India as the mantra, Sheikh Abdullah had launched the Quit Kashmir agitation against the Maharaja. It was in him that Nehru had reposed his trust and got four members nominated—Abdullah himself, together with Mirza Afzal Baig, Maulana Masoodi and Moti Ram Baigra. It was this clique that had supported 306A when it came up for inclusion in the draft constitution.

With such a notorious background, one can easily imagine how illogical it was to continue with such a discriminatory article. In order to further strengthen Article 370 came another provision, Article 35A. Article 35A too found its way into the Constitution in 1954 in an unconstitutional and surreptitious manner, by bypassing the procedure for amending the Constitution as stipulated in Article 368. Article 35A was inserted not through parliamentary assent, which is mandatory for amendments, but through a presidential proclamation.

All this was happening under Nehru, whom the apologists never tire of projecting as a quintessential democrat. The credit goes to B.R. Ambedkar for inserting Article 370 in Part XXI of the Constitution of India, which is titled 'Temporary, Transient and Special Powers'.

The Opposition's argument that Article 370 was a link to the state's accession to India is fallacious. The state's accession had concluded on 26 October 1947, when Hari Singh signed the Instrument of Accession. Article 370, according to Ayyangar's own words, took birth as a temporary provision because of the 'special circumstances' in the state. The criticism by Congress is even more specious because it is this party that has effected at least 44 amendments to this article in almost as many years.

This article had remained as an anachronism in our polity providing irrationally special powers to one state, which were being thoroughly misused by the regional leaders and parties. If

Article 370 has benefitted anybody in all these years, it is only the political leadership in the state. While the people have suffered from a lack of development, progress and prosperity, the leaders enjoyed a lack of accountability and enriched themselves. The last major industry to come into J&K was in the mid-1950s.

On the other hand, Article 370 had also become an instrument in the hands of the separatist and anti-national forces to propagate a lie that J&K was special and perpetuate sentiments of separatism in the Valley. Putting an end to this article was the much-needed measure for the complete emotional integration of the people of J&K with the Indian Union.

The decision to bifurcate the state is also a strategically shrewd move. It will insulate Ladakh from the happenings in the other two regions and provide for greater development of the region. The situation emerging in the western neighbourhood and the possible re-ascendance of the Taliban in Afghanistan call for greater attention and care to be taken in what will remain as J&K after bifurcation. Making it a Union Territory with a legislature makes a lot of strategic sense.

Barry Posner and James M. Kouzes wrote in *The Leadership Challenge: How to Make Extraordinary Things Happen in Organizations*, 'You say yes, when others say no; you do what others will not; you blaze trails; you always step up to a challenge; you make it happen; you raise the bar on what is possible; you are strong and powerful; you are a leader.' That is the kind of leadership we see in Narendra Modi and Amit Shah.

12

Kashmir
The End of Victimhood Politics

Article 370 is gone. The country is rejoicing. But there are some mourners, not just in the Valley's political circles but in Lutyens' Delhi circles as well. For some, it is an ideological confusion while for some others, it is a political compulsion. But a sane examination of the Article tells us how imperative it was for the Article to go.

We are talking about the travesty of an Article that became part of the Indian Constitution in 1950 along with more than 390 other Articles, but didn't allow these to be applied to Jammu and Kashmir (J&K). When the Indian Constitution came into force on 26 January 1950, while it was fully applicable to the entire country, only two articles of it, Articles 1 and 370, were allowed to be extended to J&K. Through Part III of the Constitution of India every Indian secured a set of Fundamental Rights that he or she enjoys unhindered (except when they were suspended by Indira Gandhi during the infamous Emergency). However, even this Part was denied to the people of J&K, courtesy of Article 370. We are talking about the Article which denied Fundamental Rights to the people of J&K. It took several years before a good number of basic Articles of the Constitution could be extended to the people of that state.

We are talking about an Article that created a major emotional wedge between the people of J&K and the rest of the country. It took four years to extend Part III of the Indian Constitution to J&K when, in 1954, a presidential order was issued applying large parts of the Indian Constitution to J&K. But then, even that was done through a sleight of hand. A new clause was inserted into the Constitution, Article 35A, by a surreptitious move.

Surreptitious, because the amendment to the Constitution, which mandates the consent of Parliament, didn't take that route. Instead, it was inserted into the Constitution through a simple presidential order. As a result, it couldn't be included in the main body of the Constitution, and was hence included in the Annexure. Technically, it is a clause in the Constitution under Article 35, but it will be found only in the Appendix to the Constitution. This itself proves the illegitimacy of said clause.

The presidential order of 1954, while extending the Union of India's laws to the state of J&K also ceded a lot of space to the state administration. The roots of this order lie in an agreement reached between then Prime Minister Jawaharlal Nehru and the leader of the National Conference in J&K, Sheikh Abdullah. This agreement came to be known historically as the Delhi Agreement. Its terms were announced by Pandit Jawaharlal Nehru in Lok Sabha on 24 July 1952, and in Rajya Sabha on 5 August 1952.

Under this agreement, Nehru had conceded enormous space to Sheikh Abdullah's whims, even to the extent of allowing the state to retain a separate prime minister, separate flag and separate constitution. It must be remembered that before their accession to the Indian Dominion in 1947, almost all the princely states of India had such arrangements. But once they merged with India, the princely states all voluntarily accepted the Indian Constitution in toto. That was not the case with J&K. While the legislatures of the princely states passed resolutions submitting themselves to the Indian Constitution and abolishing their state laws, J&K refused to do so. Sheikh Abdullah got J&K to constitute a new Constituent Assembly in 1951 and had it pass a resolution stating explicitly that J&K would retain its constitution and separate identity. Abdullah was explicit in his speech to the J&K Constituent Assembly on 5 November 1951 about its mandate. It included deciding about the future of the state too. He enlisted three alternatives for the state's future to be decided by the Constituent Assembly: accession to India, accession to Pakistan and complete independence.

According to him, even after the state's accession in 1947—even after it became a part of the First Schedule of the Indian Constitution—the accession was not final and the J&K Constituent Assembly retained the power to decide on it. Remember, we are talking about Article 370 which gave him this power to deny the application of the Indian Constitution to the state.

Nehru entered into the Delhi Agreement with Sheikh Abdullah under these circumstances. Sheikh Abdullah was able to extract maximum independence from Nehru through the agreement. Some of the clauses came to mean the following: First, while all the other states would be ruled as per the Indian Constitution, J&K would retain its constitution of 1939 and the state's newly formed Constituent Assembly would look into making necessary amendments to it in order for it to be compatible with the Indian Constitution. Power of legislation would be with the state legislature only, not with the Union

Parliament. Thus, a separate constitution was allowed. Second, J&K would continue to have its own citizens, called 'state subjects' under a state law of the Maharaja since 1927. The state legislature would have the power to make laws for conferring special rights and privileges on the so-called state subjects that won't be available to other Indian citizens living in the state. Thus, a separate citizenship was allowed. Third, J&K would retain its state flag which would be on par with the national Tricolour in the state. Thus, a separate flag was accepted.

Interestingly, one of the first amendments made by the J&K Constituent Assembly in 1952 was to abolish the monarchy. Thus came to end the famed Dogra dynasty of the state. The titles of Maharaja and Yuvaraj being enjoyed respectively by Hari Singh and Karan Singh were abolished. Karan Singh was the regent of the state. His position was renamed Sadr-e-Riyasat, a post whose occupant would be elected by the state legislature and ratified by the president of India. That meant there won't be the post of governor as the Union's representative in J&K. But then, Sheikh Abdullah didn't want the nomenclature of his own post as prime minister to be changed. Hence, the Maharaja had gone but not his prime minister. Successive chief ministers of the state used to be called prime ministers until 1967.

Thus, the Delhi Agreement, which became the basis for the 1954 presidential order, had effectively facilitated a system of 'one country, two constitutions; one country, two flags; and one country, two prime ministers'. We are talking about Article 370 which led to these monstrous anomalies. We are also talking about that Article which had provided judicial immunity to the deeds of the J&K legislature in the name of enacting laws for its state subjects. We are also talking about an Article that didn't allow the full application of the jurisdiction of many institutions, such as the Supreme Court, the Comptroller and Auditor General and even the Election Commission, for several years.

It was against these dangerous provisions that the leader of the Bharatiya Jana Sangh, Syama Prasad Mookerjee, had launched an agitation under the auspices of his own party as well as the Jammu Praja Parishad. *'Ek desh mein do vidhan; ek desh mein do pradhan; ek desh mein do nishan: Nahi chalenge* (Two constitutions, two prime ministers and two flags in one country are not acceptable)', became the war cry of the agitation. Syama Prasad Mookerjee was arrested by the J&K government and incarcerated in a guest house in Srinagar for forty days—and was found dead one day.

We are talking about an Article that didn't allow Indian laws promulgated by its Parliament to be automatically extended to the state of J&K like the rest of the country. Every such Act passed by Parliament needed the consent of J&K's state legislature. In many cases, the state legislature would make its own amendments to a law before accepting it. Only recently, this had happened to even an important national law like the Goods and Services Tax (GST) Act. The amendments to the LGBT legislation, decriminalising it, were passed by Parliament but didn't pass the scrutiny of the J&K legislature subjecting the LGBT community to the same old harassment.

We are talking about an Article that didn't allow the creation of a women's commission or a minority commission in the state of J&K. In fact, this Article was inherently anti-women. For several decades, it didn't allow women freedom of choice in marriage. While men were allowed to marry any woman from anywhere—Pakistan, Afghanistan or even the US—women were not allowed to marry outside the state. Even if a Kashmiri woman married a man from the same religion, if he was from outside J&K, she would stand to lose her status as state subject or 'permanent resident'. After a lot of hassle, finally the state had amended the law, ostensibly claiming that women could retain their permanent resident status even after marrying outside the state. But it also came with a rider, that the children from such marriage wouldn't be granted permanent resident status.

We are talking about an Article that denied basic human rights to millions of people living in the state for decades. They include the refugees who came from West Pakistan at the time of Partition and migrant workers like scavengers and other manual labourers who migrated to J&K from other parts of the country. In spite of their residence in the state for several decades, they remained non-state subjects, thus effectively deprived of many privileges, such as government education, healthcare, employment, asset and land ownership, et cetera. Important laws passed by the Union Government for the welfare of the safai karmacharis—scavengers—didn't apply to the state. We are talking about an Article that deprived these sections, largely from the Scheduled Castes (SCs), their basic human rights and human dignity.

We are talking about Article 370 which has denied political rights to the people of J&K. There are thousands of refugees who live in J&K. They all face discrimination in varying degrees. The conditions of West Pakistani refugees, who migrated to the Jammu region in 1947 in the wake of Partition, are pathetic. It may be worthwhile to mention that millions poured into states like Punjab and Rajasthan as a consequence of Partition. Some of them, like Manmohan Singh and Inder Kumar Gujral, rose to become Prime Ministers of India. But West Pakistani refugees who went to Jammu about the same time couldn't even secure the status of state subject in J&K even after spending more than seven decades there. Article 370 treats them still as outsiders and thus they are denied all the rights and privileges that state subjects in J&K enjoy. Their numbers are not small; they number in hundred of thousands today—and the majority of them are from the SCs.

Reservation for the SCs and Scheduled Tribes in the legislature is a uniform right for people of those communities across the country. But Article 370 denied that right to them in J&K. After a long battle, the SCs got political reservation, whereas the STs, who constitute close to 12 per cent of J&K's population, still don't have any such reservation of seats.

Even the 73rd and 74th Amendments to our Constitution, piloted by Mani Shankar Aiyer, the Minister for Rural Development in the Rajiv Gandhi Government in 1985, were not approved by the J&K legislature. As a result, the three-tier panchayati raj system, in vogue across the country, doesn't exist in J&K. While panchayats do elect panchs and sarpanchs, they hardly have any financial and administrative power. We are talking about that Article which denies political rights to refugees, SCs and STs and comes in the way of grassroots political empowerment in J&K.

The delimitation of constituencies was undertaken in the early 2000s across India. But the J&K legislature decided not to undertake that exercise till 2026. There is an imbalance in seats in the legislature and a resultant injustice to the people of the Jammu region. For an almost identical number of voters, Jammu gets 37 seats against the Kashmir Valley's 46. Jammu has a parliamentary seat for every 1.8 million voters whereas the Kashmir Valley has a parliamentary seat for every 1.3 million. The Valley sends three MPs while Jammu sends only two. We are talking about that

Article which has perpetrated this injustice on a section of the people of J&K.

A number of important laws that Parliament and the government have promulgated for development and for people's dignity have not been extended to J&K due to Article 370. The 42nd Amendment inserted the word 'secular' in the Preamble to our Constitution. The J&K legislature refused to incorporate this word in its constitution. J&K has had its own penal code called the Ranbir Penal Code. The Indian Penal Code has not been applicable there. Laws like the Safai Karmachari Act, Right to Education Act, Prevention of Corruption Act, 1988, et cetera also haven't had any jurisdiction in J&K.

Not just political rights, but even developmental rights of the people of J&K were seriously hampered as a result of Article 370. Since the Article hasn't allowed land to be owned by non-state subjects, no major industry has gone to J&K. The last major private industry to go to J&K was a cement factory in the 1950s. The public sector unit HMT went in the 1970s, but shut shop soon after. It's a shame that only one company in J&K got listed on any stock exchange, and that too a state-owned institution called the J&K Bank. The state subject law discouraged investors from going to J&K. There are no big private hospitals there, no big private educational institutions. We are talking about that Article which denied an ordinary Kashmiri the fruits of development that people of the rest of India are reaping.

All of this was happening in the name of an imagined special status, anchored by Article 370. In fact, the Constitution didn't use the phrase 'special status' anywhere. The Article forms part of a section called 'Temporary, Transitional and Special Provisions'.

But generations were fed the false narrative of J&K's conditional accession and special status. They were not told the fact that the document signed by Maharaja Hari Singh called the Instrument of Accession was the same signed by 535 rajas and maharajas and there was nothing special about J&K. Instead, Article 370 was displayed as proof of such special status.

It was the same discriminatory Article—which denied people development, political empowerment and dignity—that was made otiose by Prime Minister Narendra Modi and Home Minister Amit Shah between 5–7 August. A pestering wound of seventy-two years has been amputated in just seventy-two hours by the Government. Even the protagonists were surprised. If it was so easy, why did it take so long, they wondered. It didn't take seventy-two years; it took one Modi to repeal it. Prime Minister Modi demonstrated that courage of conviction.

Critics argue that the people were not consulted before the decision. The fact is that the BJP and the Sangh Parivar have been talking about the repeal of the article for the last seventy years. There was a full two-day discussion in the Parliament. Members of Parliament from the Kashmir Valley were also present in the House and participated. Thus, the argument that people were not consulted doesn't hold water. Some members argued that the route of presidential order was patently illegal. What they forget is that the Article was tinkered with at least forty-five times in the past by successive governments. Interestingly, the same presidential order route was taken every time.

But a larger question begs an answer. Who was consulted when this Article was being introduced in 1949–1950? Nobody. In fact, when the proposal for drafting a special article for J&K came up, almost everybody rejected it. When Sheikh Abdullah approached the architect of our Constitution, B.R. Ambedkar, with a request to draft the law, Ambedkar flatly refused. 'Making limited application of laws made by Parliament for the state of Jammu and Kashmir would create lots of problems rather than solving,' he bluntly told Sheikh Abdullah. Nehru then entrusted the responsibility of drafting a special law for J&K to his trusted colleague from the Madras province, and a former prime minister of Maharaja Hari Singh in Jammu, N. Gopalaswami Ayyangar.

Nehru's decision was strange. Sardar Vallabhbhai Patel was handling the accession of over 535 princely states, including the difficult ones like Hyderabad and Junagadh. Nehru singled out Kashmir and handed it over to Gopalaswami Ayyangar. In other words, Nehru retained it with himself. Patel was naturally miffed and raised strong objections, stating that as the Union Home Minister he should be allowed to handle Kashmir too. Nehru responded to Patel's annoyance rather curtly: 'Gopalaswami Ayyangar has been especially asked to help in Kashmir matters. Both for this reason and because of his intimate knowledge and experience of Kashmir, he had to be given full latitude. I really do not know where the States Ministry [Patel's ministry] comes into the picture except that it should be kept informed for the steps taken. All this was done at my instance and I do not propose to abdicate my functions in regard to matters for which I consider myself responsible. May I say that the manner of approach to Gopalaswami was hardly in keeping with the courtesy due to a colleague,' he wrote to Patel on 27 December 1947.

Gopalaswami was a seasoned politician and an ardent Congressman. But even he found dealing with Sheikh Abdullah difficult. The draft article, originally called 306A, ran into trouble with Sheikh Abdullah. Annoyed, Gopalaswami threatened to resign, saying, 'Our discussion this morning, as I indicated to you, left me even more distressed than I have been since I received your last letter from Srinagar ... I feel weighted with the responsibility of finding a solution for the difficulties that, after Panditji left for the US and within the last few days, have been created, from my point of view without adequate excuse.'

Interestingly, when the draft 306A was placed before the Congress Working Committee (CWC) in October 1949 for its approval, the committee rejected it with near unanimity except for two members—Gopalaswami himself and Maulana Abul Kalam Azad. The CWC's contention was that no such special provision could be granted to any one princely state. Nehru was abroad. He was compelled to turn to Sardar Patel, seeking his intervention in convincing the CWC.

In politics, leaders sometimes follow the orders of their superiors irrespective of their personal views. As it happens now, it happened then too with Patel. Faced with the dilemma of championing a proposal in which his heart was not, or inviting criticism that he pursued policies against Prime Minister Nehru, Patel opted for the former. He was not willing to allow any bitterness to creep in at the very dawn of Independence among the top leaders of the government. He had the proposal brought back before the CWC. When members objected, Patel convinced them to honour it since it involved Prime Minister Nehru's personal prestige as he had already given his word to Sheikh Abdullah. When Nehru returned, Patel wrote to him: 'After a great deal of discussion, I could persuade the [Congress] party to accept.' Those who invoke democratic principles to criticise the Modi government's action must answer if the Article was brought in following any democratic principle.

Patel didn't live long enough to see the Article's ill effects. But in his absence, Nehru lied in Parliament in 1952 when he said: 'Sardar Patel was all the time dealing with these matters.' It surprised even Gopalaswami Ayyangar. V. Shankar, Sardar Patel's biographer, quotes Ayyangar as bemoaning, 'It is an ill-return to the Sardar for the magnanimity he had shown in accepting Panditji's point of view against his better judgment.' Shankar also writes that Patel was never in agreement with Nehru's approach and even commented: 'Nehru royega (Nehru will repent).'

After the CWC, it was the Constituent Assembly's turn to oppose it. Something very undemocratic happened in the Constituent Assembly with respect to the princely state of Kashmir at the behest of Nehru. As per the agreement, the state was to get four seats in the Constituent Assembly: two members were to be nominated by the Maharaja and two would be from the state legislature called the Jammu Kashmir Praja Sabha. The Praja Sabha had held its election in 1946. But Nehru refused to accept the nominations of either the Sabha or the Maharaja. His contention was that the Praja Sabha didn't represent the will of the people because the National Conference led by Sheikh Abdullah had boycotted it. It is true that the National Conference didn't participate in the 1946 election to the state legislature. At a time when the country was busy with the Quit India movement against the British, Sheikh Abdullah and his National Conference were busy with the Quit Kashmir movement against the Maharaja. As part of the movement, the National Conference had boycotted the 1946 election and was unrepresented in the Praja Sabha of 1946.

Nehru insisted that the four seats in the Constituent Assembly be filled by Sheikh Abdullah's nominees. When members like K.T. Shah vehemently opposed this as undemocratic, Nehru rose to defend it as the 'correct' democratic practice: 'It amazed me to hear Professor Shah propose that the so-called Praja Sabha of Kashmir should send representatives to this House ... [H]e should know that there is nothing more bogus than the Praja Sabha ... He ought to know that the whole circumstances under which the last elections were held [in 1946–47] were fantastic and farcical. He ought to know that it was boycotted by all decent people ... and the type of people who got in [the Praja Sabha] was the type who had opposed the freedom movement throughout, who had done every injury possible to the idea of freedom of Kashmir till then ... I admit that it is not desirable for any members of this House to come by nomination or be selected by some narrow process ... though the process suggested for Kashmir is not ideal, yet I do think that it is a process that has been adopted in regard to many states in India. It is a process where you get a popular government with the representative of the popular party at the head of it, recommending to the ruler that certain names should go. Even from the view of democracy, that is not an incorrect process,' Nehru argued.

Seizing the opportunity, Sheikh Abdullah nominated himself as a member and included three of his party colleagues: Moti Ram Baigra, Mirza Mohammad Afzal Beg and Maulana Mohammad Sayeed Masoodi. All the other stakeholders in the state had been excluded and the National Conference's voice became the voice of J&K in the Constituent Assembly.

Discussion on Article 306A (which became Article 370 in the final draft) was brought before the Constituent Assembly in a hurried manner just a month before the final approval of the draft Constitution. When the discussion began, several members raised serious objections. The first to object was a member of the

Communist Party from Lucknow and a renowned Urdu poet, Hasrat Mohani. 'Why this discrimination, please?' he asked Gopalaswami, to which the reply was: 'The discrimination is due to the special conditions of Kashmir. Those questioning the temporary transition of the state to Union Territory should also understand that it too was because of the special conditions in Kashmir.'

'If you grant these concessions to the Maharaja of Kashmir, you should also withdraw your decision about the merger of Baroda into Bombay and allow all these concessions and many more concessions to the Baroda ruler also,' retorted Mohani. Gopalaswami went on to provide a long explanation for the special treatment accorded to J&K. Finally, the Article found a place in the Constitution under 'Temporary, Transitional and Special Provisions'.

It was to be a temporary provision. There were several occasions during Nehru's tenure when the demand for its repeal had arisen in Parliament. Even Bakshi Ghulam Mohammad, the Prime Minister of J&K had once urged Nehru to repeal the Article. When a group of leaders called on Nehru and demanded the repeal of Article 370, Nehru did concede that the Article was not serving any purpose. India's first spy chief, B.N. Mullik, claimed that in a private conversation, Nehru made the extraordinary admission that India 'agreed with the Jana Sangh's views that Jammu and Kashmir should be fully integrated with India and was taking steps in that direction'. In Parliament, in an oral reply, he said that Article 370 had been 'eroded and Kashmir stands fully integrated'.

Prakash Vir Shastri, a Bharatiya Jana Sangh member of Parliament from Bijnour in Uttar Pradesh, had moved a private member's Bill in Parliament in 1964 on Article 370. That Bill received wide support from members cutting across party lines. Even the Congress and National Conference members were seen supporting it. Of particular interest were the speeches made by the associates of Sheikh Abdullah.

Abdul Ghani Goni from J&K, who was earlier a staunch supporter of a separate Muslim identity for Kashmir, was surprisingly aggressive in demanding repeal of the Article. 'The then Prime Minister of J&K, Bakshi Ghulam Mohammad, had moved for abrogation of Article 370, but the central government was not agreeable to it at that time. I do not know whether the central government is under the influence of the West or wants appeasement policy towards Pakistan ... they want to please their neighbours at our cost. The central government, our Congress leaders, have not done justice to the people of Kashmir. The people of Kashmir had decided once and for all that Kashmir is an integral part of India, whether there is Article 370 or no Article 370. It is only a provisional provision and a temporary provision in the Constitution which can be removed at any time. But as far as the complete accession is concerned, that is final and nobody can challenge it,' he declared during the debate.

Goni added: 'So I dispassionately appeal to the members of this House and appeal not only to the opposition members but also to the Congress members to support this Bill and get it passed and have Article 370 abrogated from the Constitution of India, so that we may also be treated as equal citizens, as good citizens of India as any other citizen. Don't treat us as second-class citizens, and don't treat us as a colony of India. We are as much a part of India as other states.'

Another member of Parliament from the state, Syed Nasir Husain Samnani, also rose to question the relevance of Article 370, saying, 'We, the people of Kashmir, never demanded that we should be treated differently. We do not want Article 370. I want to end this curse in my lifetime, for my safety, for my children's safety, for the safety of our future generations. We should have the same laws as Maharashtra, Madras, Kerala, Bengal. We did not believe in two-nation theory of Jinnah and hence we did not allow any branch of Muslim League to be formed in J&K.'

Many in the opposition today seem to be knowledge-proof and information-proof. They haven't read the history of their own parties with respect to this Article. It was destined to go because it was coming in the way of development, political empowerment and human dignity of the people of J&K, besides nurturing a sense of separatism. It needed a strong leader like Modi to take the call, which he did on 5 August.

More than a year has passed since the annulment of Article 370 on 5 August 2019. The Valley has remained largely peaceful, barring sporadic and minor incidents. Critics attribute this absence of a public outburst of anger to the deployment of security forces in large numbers, the internet blackouts or the curfew restrictions. But then, none of this is new to the people of the Valley. Armed forces and internet blackouts have been a regular feature of life in the terror-stricken areas of the Valley. Yet, in the past, people used to come out onto the streets in large numbers, pelt stones and clash with the security forces leading, on some occasions, to casualties too. In fact, 'one dead body a day' used to be the strategy of the separatist and terrorist establishment because each casualty would be used to foment more trouble. That is no longer the situation in the Valley. People seem to understand the import of this decision. The staple of separatism fed constantly in the past seems to be declining. People realise that their leaders had all along been taking them for a ride in the name of special status and separatism. That rhetoric had helped a few political families whereas the ordinary people of J&K had remained impoverished. They are no longer ready to blindly buy the victimhood narrative as in the past. They have paused to think.

That is a good sign for the future. What the Modi-Shah duo did was historic. We stopped looking at J&K through the Pakistani prism. We took the bull of separatism by its horns. It will ultimately surrender, as it drew its strength not from the people but from the self-seeking establishment in Delhi.

13

Kashmir is Ours, Also Means That Every Kashmiri is Ours

India has many neighbours. But Pakistan is different. It is a neighbour that is singularly focused on harming and harassing India, irrespective of whether it benefits or damages its own interests. One former prime minister of Pakistan had once declared that Pakistanis would eat grass in order to fight with India for a thousand years.

Dealing with such a neighbour is not easy. Not just India, other neighbours too realise this. Afghanistan's foreign ministry complained to the UN Security Council against Pakistan's direct engagement with the Taliban bypassing the Afghanistan government, saying that it not only undermines ongoing peace efforts but violates Afghanistan's national sovereignty and UNSC Resolution 1988.

In a 2019 suicide attack, twenty-seven members of Iran's elite Revolutionary Guards were killed. The chief of the Revolutionary Guards, Major General Mohammad Ali Jafari, has accused Pakistan of providing safe havens to the perpetrators. 'Why do Pakistan's army and security body give refuge to these anti-revolutionary groups? Pakistan will no doubt pay a high price,' warned Jafari.

Pakistan is today like a cantonment or a military barrack, run by its military and ISI leadership. 'The military-industrial complex was one of Pakistan's binding forces, alongside Islam, national pride, suspicion of India and America,' writes Steve Coll in *Directorate S: The C.I.A. and America's Secret Wars in Afghanistan and Pakistan*. The deadly combination of military, Islamist radicalism and hate for India has wreaked havoc for India over decades. Zulfikar Ali Bhutto had talked about bleeding India through a 'thousand cuts'. Pakistan continues with that policy, irrespective of who occupies political power, a power that is just notional, as the real power is wielded by the army and the ISI.

That Pakistan has emerged as the global epicentre of terrorism is no longer a revelation or a secret. The entire world knows about it. One can see it in the US White House statement after the ghastly attack at Pulwama on the CRPF convoy.

'The United States calls on Pakistan to end immediately the support and safe haven provided to all terrorist groups operating on its soil, whose only goal is to sow chaos, violence and terror in the region,' read the statement issued by Trump's press secretary. No ambiguity, no 'alleged', but an affirmation about the existence of terrorist groups on 'its soil'. The UNSC stopped short of naming Pakistan, but it too openly blamed the Jaish-e-Mohammed, an organisation based out of Bahawalpur, Pakistan, for the Pulwama attack.

Pakistan must be made to change. It calls for global consensus. Tragically, we lack global consensus even on the definition of terrorism. Guided by self-interest, the US and China have both ended up patronising the monster in Pakistan, namely the military-ISI establishment. The Pakistan leadership has mastered the art of doublespeak and deception.

Kashmir occupies the centrestage of this conflict as far as India is concerned. Unfortunately, India has a huge problem with the regional narrative in the Kashmir Valley that helps Pakistan enormously. That narrative is one of separatism—soft or hard depending on the situation—alienation and victimhood. Kashmiri regional satraps are not fully reconciled to the fact, even after seventy years, that they are an integral part of India and are like any other citizen of the country. They consider their relationship with India to be special, in which they had made a huge sacrifice in 1948 by choosing India over Pakistan, and hence the Indian state and people should ever be grateful to them.

Generations of Kashmiris have been fed this fallacy by the Kashmiri regional leadership. That not just J&K, but more than 540 independent kingdoms and princely states had joined India in 1947–48 under the same document called the Instrument of Accession; hence they are an integral part of the country—is not what these eminences in the Valley teach their people. Instead, to showcase their special status, they brandish Article 370 of the Indian Constitution. This Article, inserted as a temporary and transient provision, has lived far too long. It only helped perpetuate the sense of alienation and separatism in the Valley. Mind you, even though this Article is applicable to the entire state of J&K, one doesn't find alienation or separatism in its other parts, like Jammu and Ladakh. The leadership in these regions has ensured that the people there fully integrate with the rest of India.

The ordinary Kashmiri is like any other citizen, but the leaders are the ones who turn him into a terrorist or a separatist or a stone pelter. Of greater importance is to tackle these leaders in the Valley who continue to peddle the separatist narrative.

We have given them too long a rope, in the hope that the greater the engagement, the better the integration process would be. Sadly, while large sections of the Kashmiri people wholeheartedly internalised their Indianness, the regional satraps are busy stoking separatist fires. The time has come to make them irrelevant in the Valley. Just like in the other two regions of the state, the dominant narrative to be encouraged in the Valley should also be one of Indianness.

It puts the onus on the rest of the country—its leadership and people alike. The people of India must remember that when they say 'Kashmir is ours', that also means 'every Kashmiri is ours'. If he is misguided, lead him; if he is mischievous, punish him; if he is treacherous, banish him. But instill India in him. A billion plus population can't be so powerless in tackling a handful of terrorists and their masters; but the real power lies not in hating every one, but bringing them to the right way.

'*Kartum akartum anyatha kartum shakyate*'—this is how power is defined in ancient Indian wisdom. 'It will do, it will undo, and it will do otherwise'. Doing good, undoing bad and transforming bad into good is what is described as real power.

14

Are Gupkaris Listening?

Islamism, in the Kashmiri separatist movement, was largely a subtext in the past. Mainstream identity politics used to be, at least overtly, centered on an undefined idea of Kashmiriyat. The Chaks were the last Kashmiri dynasty who had fought and defeated the Mughal rulers from Delhi like Babur and Humayun. Ultimately, Akbar resorted to deceit by inviting Yusuf Shah Chak to Delhi for talks, imprisoned and exiled him to Bihar. The last Kashmiri ruler's grave is at Nalanda in Bihar, in a dilapidated condition. For the Chaks, Kashmir's struggle was not about Islam but about their political authority.

Power changed hands from the Mughals to the British and then on to the Dogras. A resistance movement to the Dogra rulers took birth through the formation of the Muslim Conference in 1931 by Sheikh Abdullah and Mirwaiz Yousuf Shah, the hereditary Islamic cleric of Srinagar. In 1938, however, Sheikh Abdullah decided to discard the explicit Muslim identity and converted it into National Conference. The immediate reason was his suspicion that the Mirwaiz and some Jammu Muslim leaders were hand-in-glove with the Maharaja.

The National Conference under Sheikh Abdullah had not displayed overt Islamist overtones although the Sheikh would invoke Islam occasionally. Kashmiri separatism and independence became the bedrock of its politics. The resolution passed at its first Working Committee in June 1938 called for amending the constitution in such a manner that 'all the progressive forces' can 'easily become members of the Conference irrespective of their caste, creed or religion'. Two years later, the Jammu Muslims had revived the Muslim Conference and started opposing the Sheikh and the National Conference.

In August 1945, when the National Conference held its annual convention at Sopore, the speakers included Jawaharlal Nehru. Former police officer A.M. Watali narrates in his memoir *Kashmir Intifada* that when Nehru was being taken in a procession in Jhelum River on boats, the Muslim Conference workers had pelted stones in protest. Many prominent Communist leaders also actively participated in that conference. The National Conference workers used to wear badges that displayed Sheikh Abdullah in the attire of Kamal Ataturk, the secular leader of Turkey after the First World War. Nehru was so convinced about the secular character of the National Conference under Sheikh Abdullah that he advised local Kashmiri Pandit community to either 'join the National Conference' or 'bid goodbye to the country'.

Even when Sheikh Abdullah launched the illegitimate Quit Kashmir campaign against the Maharaja in 1946, the arrested leaders included many prominent Hindus and Sikhs like Sham Lal Saraf, D.P. Dhar, Sham Lal Wath, Janki Nath Zutshi, Sardar Budh Singh and Sant Singh Teg. Interestingly, while Jawaharlal Nehru went to Kashmir to court arrest in support of Sheikh's illegitimate demand; Jinnah, on the other hand, strongly opposed the campaign and used the Muslim Conference against it. When Gandhi visited Srinagar in early August 1947 to persuade the

Maharaja to release Sheikh Abdullah, he too claimed that 'the Sheikh Saheb' had fired the Kashmiris of the 'predominantly Muslim' state with 'local patriotism'. He claimed that he could not distinguish between 'a Kashmiri Hindu and a Kashmiri Muslim'.

In 1996, when Farooq Abdullah became the Chief Minister, he supposedly insisted on having Ashok Jaitley as his Chief Secretary. From then till date, many good Hindu officers have been made the chief secretaries and DGPs by Farooq and later on by Omar Abdullah. In fact, when the Rochford-born Omar Abdullah contested for the parliament elections for the first time in 1998, media used to report about his inability to speak in Kashmiri. It was during the PDP-BJP government that three local officers were made chief secretaries successively.

Sadly, out of desperate political expediency, the very same mainstream leaders, forgetting their own history, are trying to inject a dangerous Islamist discourse into the state politics today. It is true that radical Islamism is growing in the Valley. Terror groups with that narrative are trying hard to gain currency. Turkey and Erdogan are increasingly finding space in this new narrative. But to exploit it for political ends by mainstream leaders is most obnoxious. The ordinary Kashmiri still largely believes in syncretism and abhors communal agendas. 'Hendis te Musalmaanas' is the phrase ordinary Kashmiri uses even today while seeking the God for good health or good life. It is like praying: 'God save Hindus and Muslims.'

When radical Islam dominated the Valley the last time in the 1990s, the Pandits became its victims and forced to leave the Valley. It didn't spare the Valley Muslims either. Pakistani Jihadists like Mast Gul had burnt down the sacred shrine of Charar-e-Sharief. Even Farooq Abdullah had to stay away from the Valley and cool his heels in London. Those trying to inject that dangerous discourse into Kashmiri mainstream politics once again must remember all this and the immense harm Gilani and the Jamaat have done to the Kashmiris themselves.

People of Kashmir have seen this expediency and deception in the past. When Sheikh Abdullah was jailed by Nehru for sedition in 1953 and the Constitution (Application to Jammu and Kashmir) Order, 1954 was issued a year later, the Plebiscite Front was formed by Sheikh. After selling separatism for twenty years, Mirza Afzal Beig, the chairman of the Front, became a signatory to a compromise formula worked out between Indira Gandhi and Sheikh Abdullah in 1975 accepting the sovereignty of Indian Constitution over the state.

When Sheikh insisted on rolling back certain changes in the Article 370, Indira Gandhi bluntly told him that 'the clock can't be turned back'. The Sheikh's son and grandson also know that the 'clock won't be turned back' now by Prime Minister Modi either. Yet they are trying to take the people of Kashmir for a ride to chase a chimera. While the Sheikh had used plebiscite and secession as the chimera for his political ends, his scions are using Islam to deceive the Valley's youth. The Plebiscite Front merged into National Conference, and Sheikh Abdullah became the Chief Minister. But the separatist fire it ignited played havoc in the 1980s and 90s. The Gupkar leaders are resorting to that dangerous game once again, this time in the name of Islam.

Philip Spratt, a British Communist intellectual, had suggested that the solution to Kashmir problem should be 'tinged with morality, but more so with economy and prudence', in which 'material interests should supersede ideological ones'. Are Gupkaris listening?

15

A Time for New Leaders

For the separatists in Kashmir, the winter chill has set in early. And it is likely to be a long haul. The heat and dust of separatism and terrorism, that had been the bread and butter of many leaders in the Kashmir Valley, seems to have lost steam. These leaders, who had consistently been fed on the staple of separatism and special status, find the new reality unfathomable. But the people of the Valley are at least thinking about it, even if they are not openly supporting the Narendra Modi Government's move to nullify Article 370 of the Indian Constitution.

Since the passing of the presidential orders bifurcating the state of Jammu and Kashmir into two union territories and nullifying several clauses of Article 370, the popular response to these two decisions in the Valley has largely been subdued. No major violence has taken place nor has there been any terror attack. Initially, there were severe restrictions on the free movement of people, including round-the-clock curfew. But, most of the restrictions have been relaxed, either partially or fully. Vehicular movement on the streets of Srinagar and elsewhere is slowly returning. Curfew has been removed in most parts. Schools and markets are open. Life is limping back to normalcy after a few days of preventive restrictions.

For people like me, who have seen the worst form of terrorist and separatist violence in the past, including the aftermath of the neutralisation of Burhan Wani, sporadic incidents of violence in a few places in the Valley are not really that serious. The valley has been quiet and peaceful.

Perhaps people have been taken aback by the turn of events. It has still not sunk in fully. The staple of separatism and special status, on which they were fed for decades, must still be causing consternation in their minds. Yet, they don't seem to be blindly buying into the other narrative anymore like in the past. They have paused and are thinking.

One reason could be the experience of the last five years. Globally, democratic politics is changing. It is the era of strong and decisive leaders who know how to mould public discourse. The Modi era in India has seen a large-scale shift in public discourse—from the pessimism of the past to optimism about the future. The Valley is not insulated from that futuristic discourse. Through the development narrative, the Modi Government has moved closer to the hearts and minds of the people in the Valley, like in the rest of the country. The merchants of separatism in the Valley's politics have missed this shift and are stuck in the old discourse, making themselves gradually irrelevant.

The formation of the first ever BJP government in the state, together with the PDP, has helped in building up this narrative in many ways. First, it has robbed the separatists and terrorists of their political mouthpiece. The PDP used to act like a political organ of the separatists in the Valley. Having aligned with the staunchly-nationalist BJP, the PDP was forced to distance itself from that narrative, less out of conviction and more out of political expediency. Today, its efforts to return to that path are no longer viewed credibly. On the other hand, being in the government for three years has helped the BJP move closer to the people of the Valley. Various sections of the Kashmiri society had an opportunity to watch the party from close quarters. I have interacted with thousands of people from all walks of life, including separatists, in the last few years. It has certainly helped in winning over significant sections of the Valley's social leadership. Today, the calmness in the Valley is partly due to those sections of the social leadership, that include, students, youths and the non-PDP, non-NC political leadership, that have engaged with the BJP and Narendra Modi over the past few years.

It is a good sign. Once they stop and think, people realise the falseness of the narrative that they have been fed all these years by leaders from the Valley and across the border. The so-called special status has only benefitted the leaders and their cohorts; its removal will bring the fruits of development to the doorsteps of ordinary citizens of the Valley. Having given conflict a chance for several decades and ending up impoverished, directionless and insecure, the people of the Valley should give a chance now to the new narrative being offered by Modi.

'The best argument against democracy is a five-minute conversation with an average voter,' commented Winston Churchill. This is a significant reality in the Kashmir Valley. The misuse of power by a handful of leaders in the Valley has left the ordinary Kashmiri in misery. But then, the best argument for democracy is also to build confidence through humane development—the Modi way. For that, Kashmir needs a new leadership, built not on the separatist narrative of the 20th century but on the development narrative of the 21st century. It is here that the investment and focus of the central government should go. Failing that will mean a return of not just the old leadership but the dreaded old narrative of separatism and conflict.

16

The Supremacy of the Indian State and Parliament

Through a Presidential Order, the Narendra Modi Government has taken the teeth out of Article 370. The government used Clause 3 of the same Article to undo it. Clause 3 empowers President to make any changes to this Article by way of a 'public notification'. It comes with a proviso that mandates recommendation of the Constituent Assembly of the state for any such action of the President.

Opposition parties and some legal minds are raising questions on the basis of this proviso. Two things need to be understood. Firstly, the Constituent Assembly has taken the form of the state legislature; and when the state is under President's rule, the powers of the state legislature automatically transfer to the President of India. Secondly, the governments in the past had affected 44-45 amendments to this Article, starting with replacing Maharaja with Sadr-e-Riyasat in 1952. On all these occasions, the same Presidential Order route was adopted. The amendments were subsequently adopted by the state legislature, and incorporated in the state's constitution. It is the same this time around, too.

Some respected members in the House have argued that Kashmir is not purely an internal issue, and it has international ramifications. In 1994, during P.V. Narasimha Rao's prime ministership, the Parliament had unanimously declared that the only outstanding issue between India and Pakistan is the status and future of Pakistan-occupied Kashmir. If it were an international issue, why was the same argument not invoked in the past when the Article was amended forty-five times?

We must overcome this Himalayan confusion that Kashmir is an international issue. We have to confidently say that it is our internal matter. We gave the state an article as a temporary provision some seven decades ago; we amended it several times, and now decided to completely undo it. Everything is the prerogative of the Indian State and the Parliament.

Some learned members tried to drag Vallabhbhai Patel into the discussion, implying wrongly that he was instrumental in bringing Article 370. One member went to the extent of saying that Patel wanted Kashmir to be given away to Pakistan. There can't be a bigger lie than this.

Firstly, Patel had not dealt with the Kashmir matter at all. He was preoccupied with Junagadh and Hyderabad after completing the task of integration of over 535 princely states in the Indian dominion. Legally speaking, Kashmir too should have gone to him. But as mentioned earlier, Prime Minister Jawaharlal Nehru decided that a leader from Madras province, N. Gopalaswami Ayyangar, who had worked as the prime minister under the Maharaja of Kashmir, would handle it. Patel was not happy, and conveyed his reservation to Nehru.

Upset, Patel decided to resign. Gandhiji intervened. Those Congress leaders invoking Patel's name must remember that when the question of providing special status to Kashmir came up before the Congress Working Committee in 1948, no leader, except Abul Kalam Azad and Ayyangar, was in favour of it. Nehru was in the US. He had to turn to Patel with a request that he should intervene and convince the party organisation.

In politics, leaders sometimes follow the orders of their superiors irrespective of their personal views. That being the history, efforts to distort it on the sacred floor of the House are most intriguing. 'I don't want future generations to curse me that these people when they got an opportunity, didn't do it and kept this ulcer in the heart of India,' said Sardar Patel on 13 September 1948, in the context of his bold action in Hyderabad. Narendra Modi and Amit Shah must have thought the same way when they decided to bring in this historic amendment.

17

Roots and Rights in Assam after NRC

> Probably the most important event in the province during the last 25 years—an event, moreover, which seems likely to alter permanently the whole feature of Assam and to destroy the whole structure of Assamese culture and civilization—has been the invasion of a vast horde of land-hungry immigrant.

This was the warning given by British Census Superintendent C.S. Mullan as early as 1931 about the influx into Assam.

Toward the Partition of India, this influx acquired humongous proportions. It was no longer just a migration for economic reasons. It acquired political and communal overtones. As it became clear that India would be partitioned on communal lines, interested groups started aggressive campaigns to alter demography, especially in vulnerable areas like Assam.

Syed Saadulla was the Prime Minister of Assam during 1939–46. He was convinced that Assam should become a part of East Pakistan. He aggressively promoted migration of a large number of Muslim peasants and workers from Sylhet and other areas of Bengal into Assam. He deceptively called it 'Grow More Food' campaign. Lord Wavell, the then Viceroy, aptly described it as 'Grow More Muslim' campaign. The demography of Assam changed rapidly with large parts in Lower Assam becoming dominated by these migrants.

As a result, when the infamous Cabinet Mission Plan was drafted, Assam and Bengal were earmarked as Group C states allowing them to be shared between the new countries taking birth after Partition. Had leaders like Gopinath Bordoloi, the then senior-most Congress leader in Assam, with the overt support of Mahatma Gandhi, not fought back, several areas in Assam, if not the entire state, would have become a part of East Pakistan.

Partition of India was followed by massive influx of populations into both the countries. Looking at the seriousness of its impact on the future of Assam, Prime Minister Nehru called for preparing a list of Indian citizens in the state in 1950. The Immigration (Expulsion from Assam) Act, 1950 was promulgated, which started the initiative called the National Register of Citizens. A list of citizens was prepared with diligence in Assam. Unfortunately, it was never completed.

Waves of infiltration continued. In 1967, when the Prevention of Infiltration from Pakistan (PIP) Act was repealed, a large migration began. It continued through the war years of 1971–72 and thereafter. It became a major threat to Assamese demography.

'Demography is destiny,' said French Sociologist Auguste Comte. Assam's culture, traditions, lands and livelihood came under severe threat due to this unending influx. The infiltrators have occupied fertile lands of Assam. They have not even spared national parks, including Kaziranga National Park. The illegal settlements of the infiltrators had led to major violence in the Bodoland Territorial Area Districts (BTAD) when the Bodos violently attacked the infiltrators leading to a large number of deaths. Violence continued for months. Infiltration has become a major livelihood issue also. All small jobs are being taken away by the infiltrators causing severe economic hardships to the citizens of Assam.

They even started influencing the state's political destiny. The 1978 by-elections to Mangaldoi parliamentary constituency, which were announced owing to the demise of the elected MP Hiralal Patowary, became a shocking eye-opener for people of the state and the entire country. When a new voters' list for the constituency was released, people were aghast to see more than 70,000 new names being added to it. They were largely the infiltrators allegedly brought in by the Congress party in order to capture the seat. It led to widespread protests and finally culminated in the birth of the historic Assam agitation in 1979 against illegal infiltrators led by the newly formed students' association called the All Assam Students Union (AASU).

The Assam agitation received widespread support from various political and non-political sections of not only Assam but the entire country. After a six-year bloody agitation that saw the martyrdom of over 778 youth of Assam, the famous Assam Accord was signed in 1985 by governments of India and Assam, and the leaders of AASU and Asom Gana Parishad (AGP).

One of the central commitments under the Assam Accord was to prepare a National Register of Citizens (NRC) for Assam. The agitating groups had demanded that the goal of such an exercise should be to detect, delete and deport illegal infiltrators. Preparing the NRC was to be the first step helping detect infiltrators; it was to be followed by disenfranchising them and finally deporting them.

After signing the Assam Accord, both the Centre and the state governments led by the AGP did little in the direction of initiating the process for the NRC. It took another three decades for it to finally become a reality.

What was unfortunate was that even the Assamese leadership had lacked the courage of conviction to take it forward. A half-hearted effort was made in 2010 when two tehsils in Lower Assam—one each in Barpeta and Kamrup districts—were selected for a pilot project for the NRC. Violent protests by infiltrator mobs in which government offices were targeted led to deaths of several people in police firing and rattled the state government led by Tarun Gogoi. The exercise was immediately shunned and never revived by Chief Minister Gogoi.

The Supreme Court had taken a proactive interest in the matter and ordered for preparation of the citizenship rolls in December 2013. The Court had announced that the process of preparing the NRC would be monitored by it directly. Fortunately, soon after the Supreme Court's directive, the BJP came to power both at the Centre as well as in the state. Both the governments extended full cooperation, with the Centre pitching in with overall implementation through the Registrar General of India (RGI) while the state on its part provided the required staff—over 30,000 regular and 15,000 contractual employees.

In four years, something that was thought to be impossible became a reality. On 31 July 2019, the RGI released the final draft containing the names of 28,983,677 citizens of Assam. As many as 4,070,707 applicants were left out as their citizenship credentials couldn't be confirmed.

When the draft NRC was released, certain political parties started making wild allegations. It is a travesty that the very same people were once seen shouting from rooftops about illegal infiltration and its consequences. But such is the nature of our politics that the very same people are today siding with infiltrators.

It may be worthwhile to recall that P.M. Sayeed, as Minister of State for Home Affairs in P.V. Narasimha Rao's government, had categorically stated in Parliament in 1995 that lakhs and lakhs of infiltrators are entering into India from across the neighbourhood. In 1997, the then Home Minister and veteran CPI leader Indrajit Gupta had stated that more than one crore infiltrators had entered India and settled down across the country, especially in large numbers in states like Assam, Bengal and Bihar. Even Mamata Banerjee, seen today vociferously defending infiltrators, had rushed into the well of Parliament in 2005, thrown her shawl at the Speaker and accused the then CPM government in West Bengal of turning a blind eye to infiltrators and converting them into their vote bank.

The problem is known to every politician. But vote-bank politics has silenced them. The BJP, having championed the cause from the days of the Assam Agitation, has actively supported the Supreme Court initiative.

The allegation that the NRC was directed at a particular minority community is baseless. No official data on the basis of religion has been collected during the entire process. The NRC preparation was a transparent and scientific exercise. It was mammoth by any standards in the world. Over twenty completely new digital programmes were written to process 3.29 crore applications. Besides the NRC data of 1951, which was in a dilapidated condition and digitised through a laborious process, voters' lists before 1971 were also made basic documents for proof of citizenship. Besides, more than a dozen other documents, including school certificates and marriage certificates, were also permitted as proof. Proof of self or parents residing in any part of India before the cut-off date too was sanctioned as documental evidence. More than 6.5 crore such supporting documents had to be verified at the source, which was a gigantic task. Each document was sent to its source and got verified by the issuing agency. More than 2,500 NRC Seva Kendras were set up to help the applicants.

The very fact that while the citizenship cut-off year for the entire country is the 1951 Census, another two decades were allowed for Assam under the NRC, making 24 March 1971 as the cut-off date. It demonstrates that migrants, whether legal or illegal, were given two decades of grace time. That itself proves that the exercise is not directed against any community or religious group.

No country allows illegal migrants on its soil. The US, with enormous resources at its disposal, is building a fence along its border with Mexico to stop infiltrators. Even a Muslim country like Saudi Arabia regularly deports thousands of illegal migrants from fellow Muslim countries like Pakistan and Bangladesh. Interestingly, Bangladesh itself is facing a major problem of Rohingya infiltration these days. Over a million Rohingyas have illegally crossed into Bangladesh and a majority of them are residing in relief camps supported by many countries including India. Bangladesh's foreign ministry is in talks with the Myanmar government for the repatriation of Rohingyas. In fact, a team of officials from Bangladesh had recently visited villages in Rakhine province of Myanmar to oversee arrangements for repatriation.

In India, any effort even to identify infiltrators meets with political resistance. Undaunted, the Modi Government is going ahead with the NRC process and also with the process of identifying Rohingya infiltrators from Myanmar in various Indian cities for deportation.

The NRC is yet to cross several bridges. What was released was only a draft register. The Government shall ensure that no genuine citizen is denied his or her rights. Standard operating procedures are in place to ensure that people who migrated from any other part of the country are automatically included in the register. For the remaining, ample time has been given for complaints and corrections. People missed out in the draft NRC can go back with their renewed claims. They will be thoroughly verified and the final NRC will be notified only after that.

Once the final NRC is notified, those who don't find their names in that shall technically become foreigners. Even then, they will have the option of approaching Foreigners Tribunals functioning in Assam for redressal. There are 100 such tribunals already functioning there, and the Union Home Ministry is contemplating increasing their number manifold based on the final figures. Failing to prove citizenship before the tribunals is also not going to be the end of the road. Such foreigners can approach the high court. Such a long rope is being given only to ensure that no genuine Indian citizen is denied his right to be included in the NRC.

The Government is faced with the challenge of those who come to India as refugees due to persecution or general hardships of the minorities in Pakistan (including Bangladesh), Afghanistan, et cetera. This challenge was faced during the first NRC in 1950 itself. Prime Minister Jawaharlal Nehru was categorical that India is duty-bound to accept those refugees. While drafting the Immigration (Expulsion from Assam) Act, 1950, which formed the basis for the NRC, Nehru made sure that the plight of the minorities from the erstwhile East Pakistan was taken into account. The Act had explicitly said that it would not apply 'to any person who on account of civil disturbances or the fear of such disturbances in any area now forming part of Pakistan has been displaced from or left his place of residence in such area and who has subsequently been residing in Assam'. This was how a distinction was sought to be made between economic-political migration and migration of the persecuted minorities. This distinction forms the basis for the proposed Citizenship Amendment Bill 2015 of the Government of India, which applies to the entire country.

The NRC has been a major commitment of the BJP and its ideological parivar for many decades. Finally, the first decisive actions were initiated by the Modi Government to fulfil this commitment. Ensuring security of the country, and securing economic, political and cultural rights of the people of Assam are the main objectives behind this path-breaking exercise.

18

A Different Leader

In the last two years, the Indian army has repeatedly foiled attempts by Pakistan-sponsored terrorist groups to infiltrate into India. Ninety-seven terrorists were gunned down in 2015, of whom 59 were Pakistanis. The number has crossed 110 in the last eight months. Again 84 of them were of Pakistani origin. At least 17 attempts by the infiltrators were foiled by the army in the last eight months.

As is said, the terrorist has to be lucky just once, whereas the security forces have to be lucky every time. Despite best efforts by our security forces, the country couldn't escape a couple of incidents of terror at Pathankot and Uri. The important point to bear in mind is that at a time when terror has struck many European and American cities, India has largely remained terror-free in the last couple of years. It is a well-known fact that Prime Minister Narendra Modi has made sincere and genuine efforts to convince the neighbour of the futility of supporting, sponsoring and launching terror. He met Pakistan's then Prime Minister Nawaz Sharif a couple of times. He made an impromptu visit to Lahore on his way back from Kabul. The two prime ministers met in Russia and decided to have a three-tier dialogue process set in motion between the two countries.

But then came the infamous Pathankot attack, where the Pakistani terrorists had succeeded in penetrating into the Indian Air Force base and held on for close to seventy-two hours, until they were neutralised. Pathankot was the first major terror challenge thrown at PM Modi by Pakistan. The Indian government had tried one last time to deal with it in the conventional manner. It went so far as to even allow Pakistani investigators access to parts of the attack site.

Despite the Indian government's overtures, Pakistan remained a nation committed to terror, lies and denial. Sadly, it allowed an olive branch extended by PM Modi to lapse. It didn't realise that it was dealing with a different leader and a different government. Pathankot and the aftermath was the proverbial last nail. Any further misadventure from Pakistan was to receive a tough response from India. Uri was more than a misadventure by Pakistan. Killing eighteen soldiers inside a military camp situated a couple of kilometers inside the LoC is nothing short of a war crime. If terrorism becomes the state policy of a rogue nation, victim countries are left with very few options. Uri too has left India with very limited options.

More than the military might, it was the political will that was challenged. When I used the phrase, 'For one tooth the entire jaw', at one level, I was giving vent to the strong popular anger and resentment, but at another level it meant that the government should now go all out to end this menace. The prime minister had on day one made it clear that this time the perpetrators shall 'not go unpunished'. In a way, barring the usual gang of peaceniks and mombattiwalas, largely the country and the government were on the same page with regard to responding to this misadventure by Pakistan.

Normally, it couldn't have come at a more difficult time—the United Nations was in session. But the Indian government saw an opportunity in this difficulty. A multi-pronged action plan was quickly put in place wherein a diplomatic offensive was launched together with a publicity overdrive.

India's aggressive response to Prime Minister Nawaz Sharif's lies at the UN was a clear indicator of the things to come. It didn't mince words, called Pakistan the host of 'the Ivy League of terror', described it as the 'global epicentre of terrorism' and finally the young IFS lady officer, exercising the right of reply, thundered, 'What we see in Pakistan, Mr President, is a terrorist state.'

Naming and shaming Pakistan globally, isolating it on the diplomatic front and acting against terror targets were all a part of the multi-pronged strategy devised by the government. Leaving behind the policy paralysis of yesteryears and the so-called 'strategic restraint', the prime minister has taken the battle deep inside the Pakistan territory by talking to the people of that country directly.

In his Kozhikode address, the prime minister had spoken about the need for both the countries to fight against hunger, illiteracy and backwardness; but he had not precluded action against Pakistan. In fact, he told the Indian army that 1.25 billion Indians were behind it and repeated his earlier statement that he wouldn't let the perpetrators of the Uri attack escape punishment. Some peaceniks wanted to read a different message in it. Some of those who were sworn adversaries of Prime Minister Modi, started penning blogs too, praising Modi's 'restraint'. But before their ink could dry, the operations against the terrorists waiting at the launch pads across the LoC in PoK were successfully completed by the Indian Army in a midnight operation.

Uri has changed India-Pakistan relations significantly. They will no longer be the same for at least some time to come. Nobody wants war; but the alternative to war is peace; not humiliation and terror attacks. The rants of some Pakistan ministers about the nuclear first-use show the rogue nature of that country, which is the worst proliferation in recent years. Nobody wants nuclear war, but the world can't be a mute witness to the nuclear blackmail of rogue nations.

Terrorism is a global cancer. It needs surgical intervention. India has done its part. It will continue to defend its borders and citizens from this menace in the same manner. But it is also time the world community exerts pressure on Pakistan; pressure not just to ask Pakistan to 'behave', but as former External Affairs Minister Sushma Swaraj exhorted at the UN, 'if it doesn't behave, throw it out of all international fora'. That has already happened at the SAARC. For Pakistan, terrorism has come as a cheaper option all these years. Time to make it costly for it.

19

A People's Idea

'Ekah Shabdah Samyagjnatah Suprayuktah Loke Swarge cha Kamdhuk Bhavati'—one word used at the right time and right context will come in handy in this life and beyond.

This Patanjali sutra aptly applies to the controversy over my views on Akhand Bharat. Something that was stated and restated several times before by several people in the Parivar became an issue only because it came at a time when Indo-Pak ties were in for a path-breaking initiative by Prime Minister Narendra Modi.

I did an interview for Al Jazeera on 7 December. A question was put to me about the Akhand Bharat map in the Nagpur headquarters of the RSS. Like on many other occasions, I answered that the RSS had held the view that one day there would be a reunion of all the three parts through popular will and consent. I also made it clear twice that it wouldn't be through armies or aggression but only through popular goodwill. All that it meant was that it would be a people's reunion at the cultural and societal level.

Coincidentally, the airing of the interview happened on the very day Prime Minister Modi had made an important visit to Lahore to greet Nawaz Sharif and his family. In a tweet I said the following about that visit: 'PM Modiji's sudden stopover at

Lahore to greet Pak PM Nawaz Sharif is a much needed departure from protocol-driven politics between the two countries. Like leaders of EU, ASEAN and even countries in our neighbourhood, leaders of India and Pakistan too needed to inject informality in their relations. What better day than the birthday of Atalji for this path-breaking departure.'

I feel sad that my interview was used to diminish the importance of the Prime Minister's path-breaking gesture. We in politics need to look at the immediate—at the most, the next three, four, or five years. Some of us who have imbibed the generational vision of the RSS tend to get trapped in political incorrectness.

Let me reiterate that the Akhand Bharat doctrine is a cultural and people-centric idea. I was not even remotely suggesting that we should redraw the boundaries of our countries. But I do notice great eagerness and urge among the people in all the three countries for greater engagement and interaction. In fact, more than me, it is the seculars and mombattiwallas who have been highlighting this urge by talking about open borders and organising candlelight demonstrations at the Wagah border.

The Partition of 1947 has created a political divide. Who was responsible for it, is a historical debate. In his book, *Guilty Men of India's Partition*, Lohia held the three main players—the British, Congress and Muslim League—responsible for it. Later historians have argued about others too.

Speaking about the acceptance of Partition by the Congress, Nehru told Leonard Mosley in 1960: 'The truth is that we were tired men and we were getting on in years too. Few of us could stand the prospect of going to prison again and if we had stood out for a united India as we wished it, prison obviously awaited us. We saw the fires burning in Punjab and heard every day of the killings. The plan for Partition offered a way out and we took it'.

However, was Partition also a divide of the people? In the heat of it, probably a large number of people on both sides got emotionally identified with the new political identity. That political identity will continue to remain. But there is another broader identity of a society that has lived on for millennia as one. Eminent historian Ayesha Jalal, in her book on Manto and Partition, eloquently highlights this dilemma by invoking the idea of a cultural nation, 'The extent to which the contours of the cultural nation, creatively and broadly construed, do not map neatly onto the limited boundaries of the political nation.'

In fact, Saadat Hasan Manto, one of the best storytellers of the 20th century, was among those on the Pakistan side who had never reconciled with the idea of the people splitting. One of his Partition stories that Jalal refers to was 'Toba Tek Singh' in which the non-Muslim patients of a mental asylum in Lahore agitatedly await relocation to India because of their religious affiliation. 'Portraying the inmates to be of sounder mind than those making the decisions for their removal, Manto deftly questioned the wisdom of Partition and the sheer madness it had let loose,' comments Jalal.

That being the case, can we come together as people? Can we cherish the historical, civilisational reality that we had been one people with a shared history for millennia? When I said 'through popular goodwill and consent', this is what I meant.

When Jesus was made to stand before Pontius Pilate for trial, he asked the accusers to define their words first so that there is no confusion in the arguments. That is probably the case with Akhand Bharat too.

In the early 1960s, socialist and Jana Sangh leaders, Ram Manohar Lohia and Deendayal Upadhyaya, came closer to each other. Dr Lohia told Deendayalji that the Jana Sangh's and RSS's belief in the concept of 'Akhand Bharat' put Muslims in Pakistan at unease and posed a hurdle in the progress of Indo-Pak relations. Lohia said: 'Many Pakistanis believe that if the Jana Sangh came to power in New Delhi, it would forcibly reunify Pakistan with India.' Deendayalji replied: 'We have no such intentions. And we are willing to put to rest Pakistani people's concerns on this score.' Out of those interactions between the two was born the idea of an India Pakistan Federation.

As pointed out by BJP spokespersons, Atalji, during his historic bus yatra in 1999, made it categorically clear that India and Pakistan are two sovereign nations. I and many like me strongly hold the view that the coming together of India, Pakistan and Bangladesh as people, on the basis of mutual goodwill and shared common historical ties, is a very important step to overcome our strained political relations. I am anguished that my essentially ideological position has been misconstrued to be the political programme of my party or the government of the day.

20

Strategic Culture

India has earned the sobriquet 'Soft State' due to its handling of terrorism and hostile neighbours over the years. After the hanging of Ajmal Kasab, the terrorist responsible for Mumbai attacks in 2008, some commentators opined that India has now shed the image of a Soft State. Is it true?

There is no denying the fact that the decision of the government to hang Kasab after his mercy plea was rejected by Hon' President Shri Pranab Mukherjee has certainly given a sense of relief to the people of the country. After all we brought one dreaded terrorist to justice, they felt. The government, and especially Shri Pranab Mukherjee, must be complimented for their swiftness and boldness.

However, it will be premature to conclude that we have shed the Soft State tag completely. Actually, it is not about just a couple of decisions. Demands arose, correctly, that the other dreaded terrorist who was responsible for the carnage at the Parliament building in December 2001, Afzal Guru, be also executed immediately. Following the rejection of a mercy petition by the President of India, he was executed on 9 February 2013.

These decisions are in a way inevitable ones. The judicial process was duly completed and the government is only expected to follow the procedures in these cases. But for us to change our image we need to do a lot more. The opposite to Soft State is not hard or harsh State. What we need is a stern State, a polity that betrays zero tolerance to attacks on its sovereignty, dignity and integrity.

Countries like Israel, the US and even Russia display such attitude. It is in their culture. Israel is by culture driven by fight back instinct. It is not 'teeth for teeth' with them; 'for one tooth, the entire jaw'. That is the reason why in spite of being surrounded by the enemy five times larger in terms of demography and military strength and sworn to wipe out Israel from the map of the world, they not only merely survive, but lead a life of strength, courage and pragmatism.

India is driven by an instinct of compromise. We may pay lip sympathy to Gaza by asking Israel not to use disproportionate force; but one has to be on the other side of the Gaza border to understand what it means to be a target of Hamas terrorism. Everything is fair in love and war, they say. We ourselves were victims of excessive softness in 1962 when waves and waves of Chinese soldiers had invaded our territory outnumbering our soldiers by 1:6. Excessive force argument doesn't have any merit in a war; and Israel is in a perpetual war.

In the US, terrorists are tried in military courts and punished swiftly. Mind you, the US is one of the world's leading democracies. Russia cannot claim that honour, but when it comes to handling terror, Putin had demonstrated extreme commitment when he carpet-bombed Chechnya relentlessly for a month to finish off Islamic terrorism once and for all on Russian soil.

Our real problem lies in the lack of that courage and determination. We are driven by a romanticist attitude of peace and love, when what we actually need is a strategic culture. When Nehru proposed Panchsheel—five principles for peaceful coexistence—to Zhou Enlai, Mao retorted by saying what we needed was 'armed coexistence'.

That is what is meant by the strategic cultural difference in thinking. It is not about any doctrine alone. It is more about the culture. We simply don't have it. The last known leader to have thought in terms of a comprehensive strategic cultural doctrine was Chanakya when he asked the ruler of Patna to go and befriend the rulers of the Republics in today's Afghan-Iran border thousands of miles away. There were kings like Shivaji who had used strategic wars to secure their kingdoms, but a strategic doctrine leading to a strategic culture was last developed by Chanakya in *Arthashastra*, which we no longer follow.

Let me give you a simple example to buttress my point: in order to secure its borders from the Mongol invaders in the North the Qing dynasty in China had built the Great Wall of China—a thousands-of-kilometre-long wall around its central territory after 13th century. India was invaded by successive waves of hordes for more than 2000 years through one mountain pass called the Khyber Pass. Why has no Indian king ever thought of sealing that pass to prevent the invasions?

That is where the difference in strategic cultures stand. That is why we can't even seal our borders with Bangladesh. Even if we post our BSF men there, we give them clear orders that they cannot fire on the infiltrators even at night.

For us to really shed off this Soft State image we need to transform our cultural outlook about our security, sovereignty and national honour. We need a new strategic culture in our country.

A VIEW FROM WITHIN

'Today, our attempt is not to rectify history. Our only aim is to proclaim anew our attachment to the faith, convictions and to the values on which our religion has rested since immemorial ages.'
—Rajendra Prasad

21

Gentle, Yet Atal

Atal Bihari Vajpayee was an accomplished journalist and poet, orator par-excellence, a true party karyakarta, a disciplined swayamsevak and along with all these he was a gentle and lovable human being. Atal ji was an institution in himself. Whoever came in contact with him, certainly came back as an enriched person. He left an indelible imprint on the life of thousands if not millions through his personality as well as politics. With his demise, a political era marked neither by competition nor conflict, and nor even power-friendly politics, but by conciliation has come to an end.

In Bhagavad Gita, it is said whoever is born shall die. But the mother earth and humanity shall be poorer by the passing away of statesmen like Atalji. Some called him a fatherly figure, some called him a statesman, some said he was a true democrat, for some he was a man of speech, for some he was Babji. Lata Mangeshkar called him Dada. Americans remember him through his description of the US-India relationship as natural allies. Chinese remembered him as the only Indian leader to have met three successive generations of the Chinese leadership starting with Mao Zedong to Deng Xiaoping to Hu Jintao. Bangladeshis remember him for his contribution in the liberation war. Many would not know that Atalji was presented with the highest Bangladesh Liberation War Honour. Even the Kashmiri separatist leaders remember him as one who sincerely wanted to resolve the Kashmir problem. Atalji's demise is an irreparable loss to contemporary India.

Atalji practised a version of politics that is rare to find today. His politics of love to the nation took precedence over the love of power. It was politics in which feelings, sentiments, emotions found a place in the world of cutthroat competitive politicking. Atalji practised a different version of politics which involved not disrespecting adversaries, not rejection of others, and not politics of name calling.

His life was an open book and he led a transparent life. He was the same within and outside. His personal and political life was an open book like that of Gandhi. Everybody loved him and cared for him and admired his courage of conviction. Despite this, he never held himself above the party and was a true swayamsevak. He obeyed the decisions of the party as a disciplined karyakarta even at times when he did not agree with some of those. Walter Anderson, eminent political thinker, had said politics and discipline do not go together and the only exception was Atal Bihari Vajpayee.

Today though, we have done away with untouchability in social life, yet we acquired a new kind of scourge called political untouchability. No two people from two different parties see eye to eye. But Atalji practised a goodwill politics and had good words even for his adversaries, including Pandit Nehru.

While Nehru had said Atalji would occupy his position one day, Atalji had paid genuine glowing tribute to Nehru when the latter passed away. Atalji maintained this quality till the end of his life.

Atalji was compassionate towards the karyakartas. Whatever position he was in, he never displayed any arrogance. I have my own experience to narrate. In 1993, as a young man in his twenties, I was sent to interview Atalji for my magazine when he was the leader of the opposition. This was a few months after the fall of disputed structure in Ayodhya and I had a few uncomfortable questions to ask. Atalji did not get angry; instead he nudged me through the interview for fifteen minutes, giving all answers peacefully.

Though he had to rush to the Parliament and was reminded by another Minister, he said, 'Wait, I am teaching journalism to this young pracharak from Andhra Pradesh.' One of the significant initiatives of Atalji's government was to constitute a committee to look into the functioning of the Constitution. This was in 2000. The committee was portrayed in bad light by media and showcased it as a review committee while its aim was to look into the effective working of the Constitution. Dr Ambedkar gave the Constitution for the people but warned that however good the Constitution may be, if it goes into the hands of bad people, its purpose would not be served. People are the real masters.

Democracy is a direct agreement between the elector and the elected. People usually know only that part of the Constitution that affects them. Even though we promulgated the Constitution in 1950, we never made any effort to educate people about it. Thanks to Prime Minister Modi, in 2015 it was decided to observe 26 November every year as Constitution Day, so that people understand what the Constitution stands for. It is this lack of awareness among the large section of the society that is being misused by certain organisations within and from outside to wreak havoc in the country. Dr Ambedkar had warned us against such misuse. India had lost Independence due to the infidelity and treachery of some of our own people. If some of our own betray us again, we may lose Independence and be forced into slavery again and we should guard ourselves against repeating this.

Let me enumerate four major challenges. First, failure of the Constitution governance is a challenge. Among the three limbs of the Constitution, the judiciary seems to be passing through a tumultuous time.

We know that justice delayed is justice denied but few opine that justice hurried is also justice denied. In the Ram Janmabhoomi case, the Allahabad High Court had ordered the trifurcation of the disputed land. The case was brought to the Supreme Court, only to decide if the High Court order was valid or not.

However, the opposing parties posed question on the mosque being an integral part of Islam or not to delay the judgment. When it came up for consideration, the Chief Justice took just three minutes and disposed the hearing saying that it was not a priority. It was due to such a dismissal by the Supreme Court stating that the issue was not priority that we saw large-scale demonstrations across the country by the temple protagonists. People showed that it was indeed a priority by participating in lakhs all across the country.

The second challenge comes from the bureaucracy. This is about the entire system of bureaucracy and not individuals. This system has become a hurdle of development. Former President of India Shri Pranab Mukherjee himself had said this. As a system, it is unaccountable and poses a big challenge to constitutional governance. Dr Ambedkar in his speech had said that if political parties keep creed above the country, our Independence will be put in a jeopardy the second time. For Vajpayee, country was a temple, we are priests of it and we must sacrifice our lives in the service of the rashtrapurush. This was politics for Atal Bihari Vajpayee. When he was defeated in 1997 after thirteen days in power, he spoke in the Parliament and said that parties come and go, governments come and go, but the nation has to be there and democracy has to be there forever. But today, parties are shrinking and there is only one national party and rest are regional parties. The reason for this is that the identity politics is at its zenith. Identity based on caste, language or region is dictating the politics of today and this is a global phenomenon. This is a challenge for the Constitution to deliver.

Atalji was a poet. He was a man of thought. In the rustle and rumble of politics, he used to turn to poetry as a relief. He had said that his poetic heart gave him the strength to face the political problems particularly those that have a bearing on his conscience. He was a man of emotions and was humility personified. It is difficult to find humility in politics and Atalji in his poem requests God not to take him to heights where he cannot reach his own people. Atalji showed us how to accept success and failures without attitude. He used to say that one should take victory and defeat with equanimity and only a humble leader could live a life like that.

Today, it is not easy to survive in politics as it can be harsh. It is not possible to state the truth in politics. But Atalji practiced politics of honesty and accommodation. He had set an example as a politician and had no enemies. Hence, he was called 'Ajatashatru'. He was honest to himself and was transparent before the nation. He never believed that he was always right. If someone believes that he is always right, that is the starting point of hate. Atalji, through his life and politics, has been a living example for us all. With the passing away of Atalji, an era has come to an end. It is true that it is difficult to find another Atalji. But the era of politics he ushered in, the politics of positivity, politics of compassion and dignity, politics of humility will guide us forever.

22

In Atalji's Mould

What a cruel destiny it is to be forced into writing obituaries every few months. In the past five years, we in the BJP have lost six young and dedicated leaders to untimely deaths. First, it was Gopinath Munde, followed by Anil Madhav Dave, Ananth Kumar, Manohar Parrikar, Sushma Swaraj, and now Arun Jaitley. We lost our beloved Atalji too. No single political party in Indian history has faced such tragedy.

'*Jaatasya hi dhruvo mrityuhu.*' Those who are born shall die, said Lord Krishna in the Bhagavad Gita. Yet, when promising leaders pass on in their prime, we long for better answers. The void that these leaders have left behind is hard to fill.

Arun Jaitley was a gentleman politician—suave, sophisticated, humane and witty. He was not just a leader; in over three decades of political life, Jaitley had become an institution. He was our one-stop reference for everything—whether it was the challenges faced by the government or the party or questions about the nation's future or political issues. From leaders in the states to ministers in the cabinet, from the BJP's alliance partners to parties on the other side, everyone would turn to him for solutions and guidance. For the media, he was the source of information and the 'line-giver'. He was simply indispensable.

Jaitley rose through the party ranks. A find of the Atal-Advani era, he came into prominence through hard work, dedication and talent. An activist of the ABVP, he was incarcerated during the Emergency. When a lucrative offer to contest polls was in sight during the Janata Party regime, Jaitley chose to establish himself as a successful professional before taking the political plunge. A decade in the rugged terrain of the Indian legal system had probably helped him become an expert in matters of law and justice and constitutional intricacies. By the time he became an integral part of the BJP in the late 1980s, Jaitley had made a reputation as a legal and constitutional luminary. This expertise, coupled with his raw sense of grassroots politics, made Jaitley a great asset for the BJP.

Jaitley's used to be the last word on many legal and constitutional questions that the party would face in the states or at the national level. Law and matters related to the Constitution were at his fingertips. But the solutions he would provide were not just those of a lawyer or a constitutional expert, but also of a shrewd politician, who had his nose to the ground. He had an amazing understanding of the country's grassroots political reality.

Jaitley was a versatile genius. He handled the finance and defence ministries with equal aplomb. Under two prime ministers, he held portfolios as diverse as law, information and broadcasting, disinvestment, finance and defence. As the Leader of Opposition or Leader of the House in the Rajya Sabha, he led or participated in several committees and commissions, always adding great value to their functioning.

Jaitley was a quintessential democrat. If we were to name one leader as a successor of Atal Bihari Vajpayee's legacy in politics, it was him. He never believed in political untouchability. He had as many friends in the Opposition as in his party. Like Vajpayee, he too endured criticism with dignity. Like Vajpayee, Jaitley was a man of ideas, feelings and words. Atalji used poetry to express himself while Jaitley used prose. Both were superb orators. Jaitley inherited Atalji's sense of humour as well. Satire used to be a cherished ingredient in politics in the past. But of late, it has become a rarity. The exception was Arun Jaitley. A player with words, he would use puns frequently in his political discourse to score points without offending the other side. An ability to lighten a heavy debate through his ready wit was Jaitley's forte. He also had the unique ability to lift a discourse intellectually. He was one of the few leaders in Indian politics with whom one could have an intelligent and profound conversation.

Jaitley's fondness for cricket is well-known. He was an office-bearer at the BCCI and led the Delhi and District Cricket Association from the front. During his tenure, he promoted many young talents who later became star players in the Indian cricket team. In politics, he was like an all-rounder in cricket. He knew how to hit sixes for the ruling side, how to bowl out the Opposition through tough arguments and how to field the interests of his party in challenging times.

Jaitley owed his rise in politics to the Atal-Advani leadership, when young leaders were spotted and promoted by the party. During the past three decades, Jaitley too spotted, supported and promoted several young talents in Indian politics. Several leaders in today's BJP, including several in the government, owe their political rise to Jaitley.

With Jaitley, one had the freedom to disagree yet continue to have dialogue and a cordial relationship. He never saw disagreements on issues to be matters of personal prestige. He was a Kashmir specialist. He diligently guided me and Haseeb Drabu in drafting the Agenda of Alliance between the BJP and the PDP. I vividly remember how after forty days of intense deliberations, we were stuck over a couple of points. At Prime Minister Narendra Modi's advice, we approached Jaitley who was busy giving final touches to the Union Budget. He joined us outside the North Block at 1 a.m., standing on the road between South and North Block, nudging us towards closing the matter to mutual satisfaction. Arun Jaitley is no more. As songwriter Irving Berlin wrote: 'The song is ended; but the melody lingers on.'

23

Election Result
In Favour of Narendra Modi

'In the turmoil of battle, the great general maintains a psychological serenity like the needles of the compass in the storm-tossed ship', writes Clausewitz. Consciously or otherwise, the Opposition has centred this election round Modi. And the results affirm a phenomenon that Marxist social scientist William Davies describes as 'the leader becomes the truth'.

'The data suggests that the ill may have been particularly susceptible to Mr Trump's message. According to our model, if diabetes were just 7 per cent less prevalent in Michigan, Mr Trump would have gained 0.3 fewer percentage points there, enough to swing the state back to the Democrats. Similarly, if an additional 8 per cent people in Pennsylvania engaged in regular physical activity, and heavy drinking in Wisconsin were 5 per cent lower, Mrs Clinton would be set to enter the White House.'

This was not a stand-up comedian, but a highly reputed magazine from London analysing Donald Trump's victory in 2016. Many such 'expert analyses' are awaited after May 23. They blamed EVMs first, the Election Commission next, the pollsters after that, and finally, they will end up blaming the voters.

This is a completely positive mandate in favour of Narendra Modi. The sheer magnitude of the victory amazes even the seasoned political pundits. Modi has simply conquered the heart of India. Conventional political wisdom suggests that ruling parties can't create waves. It is usually the opposition that creates a wave. But PM Modi is a known convention-breaker. He has created a strong wave in his favour.

We often refer to war terminology in a lot of non-war activities these days. 'Cyber warriors', 'media wars', 'electoral battles', 'green warriors' et cetera, are descriptions that are too casually deployed to describe the activity of a given group. In that sense, elections too became like a war. They are fought with no less intensity and fervour. This was the case with the current election too.

Carl von Clausewitz, a Prussian general of the 17th century, in his book *On War* described war as 'the continuation of politics by other means'. His treatise became famous as 'Clausewitzian doctrine'. According to Clausewitz, three basic factors determine the outcome of war: The administrative element (overall strategic planning and logistics); the military element (resources and men) and the emotional element (campaign theme and tactics).

The overall strategic planning of the BJP's campaign, led by Amit Shah, has been miles ahead of the Opposition. The party had put in enormous efforts in areas where additional dividends were expected, like West Bengal, Odisha and the North East. The results in these states prove that those efforts paid off. On the other hand, the Opposition's campaign was lacklustre and bombastic.

The BJP had mobilised all its organisational resources very well. The organisational structure that team BJP put in place right up to the polling station level has played an important role in this election. The Opposition lacked in that respect too. The senior and seasoned leadership of the Congress party was less visible while the campaign was left on the shoulders of inexperienced young leaders.

Finally, the Opposition had no answer to PM Modi's strong emotional pitch. Modi effectively intermixed his personality, his developmental programmes of the last five years and the ideology in action to generate a strong emotional sentiment among the masses in his support. Those accusing Modi of using 'nationalism' for electoral ends must remember that nationalism is not just an election issue, but forms the very identity of the BJP. Modi has many achievements in the past five years to showcase, reaffirming his nationalist credentials. That is what Modi and the BJP did during the campaign. In fact, this mandate is a proud reaffirmation of the people's commitment to nationalism. It is, in a way, an answer to all those critics, both domestic and international, who called Modi a divisive figure. It is the most expansive and inclusive mandate in support of the nationalist idea of India.

Modi is a shrewd learner. He didn't hesitate to follow Napoleon, whom historian Eric Hobsbawm described as the 'secular deity', in some of his tactics. Napoleon had mastered the art of using propaganda. He ran a government newspaper, *Le Moniteur Universel*, that regularly informed the French public about his military heroics and war successes. 'What counts is what the people think as true,' Napoleon used to say. The Opposition's lies didn't cut any ice before the people's belief in Modi because of his relentless and direct engagement with them through various communication platforms.

Modi led from the front. He bore the brunt of the Opposition's attacks on himself and responded with firmness. 'In the turmoil of battle, the great general maintains a psychological serenity like the needles of the compass in the storm-tossed ship', writes Clausewitz. Consciously or otherwise, the Opposition has centred this election round Modi. And the results affirm a phenomenon that Marxist social scientist William Davies describes as 'the leader becomes the truth'.

In the end, the Opposition has been left flabbergasted. They had no answer to this unconventional and intense electoral onslaught unleashed by Modi and the BJP. '*Sesham kopena purayet*'—'Rage is the only option left'—goes the ancient Indian saying. All that the nation sees from the Opposition is illogical and irrational anger and rage.

Modi-II starts on a strong wicket. Its immediate priorities are clearly laid out. Attending to the economy is, of course, one such priority. While the macroeconomic picture looks stable and promising, many important segments need support from the government. India cannot completely remain insulated from the ongoing trade war between the US and China or the geo-strategic conflict between the US and Iran. The neighbourhood also calls for attention. Developments in Sri Lanka and relations with Pakistan need the prime minister's time and attention. Giving an impetus to the Indian Ocean strategy to secure India's economic and strategic interests needs more focus from the government in Modi-II. The kind of mandate that Modi-II has secured makes it easy for the PM to tackle many security and strategic challenges.

This mandate is significant for another reason. It has completed the rejection and decimation of what Modi himself described as the 'Khan Market cacophony' of pseudo-secular/liberal cartels that held a disproportionate sway and stranglehold over the intellectual and policy establishment of the country.

Under Modi-II, the remnants of that cartel need to be discarded from the country's academic, cultural and intellectual landscape.

Narendra Modi is seen by the people of India as not just another prime minister, but as a 'transformative leader'. Nothing short of building a New India is his goal. The road to transformation is not easy but we have already taken that road. In Modi-II, the country expects the government to tread that path with a greater vigour.

24

Glasnost in RSS

It is a Glasnost moment for the Sangh. In the mid-1980s, Mikhail Gorbachev brought in new 'openness' in the thinking and actions of the USSR. He didn't reject Communism. He insisted that there was a need for more openness and accommodation. Called Glasnost, it revolutionised the politics and geography of Eastern Europe.

What the RSS chief did through his three-day lecture series in the national capital in September 2018 is no less significant. With utmost lucidity and disarming honesty, he has certainly won over Lutyens Delhi's intelligentsia. His lectures, followed by long but equally candid question-answer sessions, have brought in freshness about the understanding of the organisation. Critics were speechless while the sceptics nodded in approval of the many profound statements he made in his speeches.

'The RSS is very difficult to understand and very easy to misunderstand,' a frustrated scholar commented about three decades ago. This frustration was shared not only by those watching the RSS from outside but also by some who observed it from within. The difficulty was largely of the RSS's own creation. Despite the fact—highlighted by Bhagwat in his speech—that the organisation's founder, K.B. Hedgewar, had wanted it to have a publicity wing as early as in 1936, the RSS largely remained a reticent and shy outfit.

'Prasiddhi Pranmukhta,' shunning popularity, is an article of faith for the RSS even to this day. It was practised with much rigour and religiosity in the first six decades. It was only in 1985—when the organisation celebrated its 60th anniversary and decided to undertake a mass contact programme—did the realisation dawn on the RSS's leaders that people were largely unaware of the organisation's inner thinking, even though it had grown into an all-India phenomenon. It endured criticism and ridicule, mostly motivated or ill-informed, but never bothered to respond. An eminent leader once likened the RSS to a tortoise: It would withdraw into its shell when attacked and spread its limbs and start walking again once the attackers left. The result was a campaign of stereotyping and vilification.

The first leader to bring in organisational openness was Balasaheb Deoras, the third RSS chief. Under his leadership, the organisation formally started reaching out to the society at large. Its three important wings—seva or service, sampark or PR and prachar or publicity—were started during that period.

Bhagwat has gone further. His three-day lecture series witnessed significant openness on the important ideological questions that the organisation has been identified with. As an insider, I am privy to the shift in the last decade or so since Bhagwat took over. He has finally spelt out this shift before the countrymen.

The most significant statement was about Hindu Rashtra and Muslims. Bhagwat used a double negative to drive home an important shift. 'No Hindu Rashtra without Muslims,' he almost declared. Double negatives help to allow various interpretations. However, the fact remains that it is a significant shift. I recall a question put to one senior RSS functionary sometime in the 1980s—'Why were Muslims and Christians not allowed to join RSS?' The leader responded with a counter-question—'Do girls schools admit boys?' 'The RSS's mission is to unite Hindus. Where is the question of inviting those who are not Hindus—by religion or culture or whatever?' From there to the above statement is quite a journey.

The same holds true for Bhagwat's candid admission that some statements from *Bunch of Thoughts* and other publications attributed to Guruji Golwalkar should be seen in the context of his times. In other words, he admitted that some of Golwalkar's statements were timed out and no longer relevant. This is refreshing openness and intellectual honesty. Gandhiji used to say, that if a reader finds any contradiction in his views, he should go by the latest one—since with time, Gandhiji may have acquired new knowledge and refined his thoughts. Bhagwat suggested that this rationale be applied to the RSS too.

Actually Bunch of Thoughts was a compilation of the speeches delivered by Golwalkar over a period of 33 years as RSS chief. He didn't author the content, nor did he give the titles. And if one goes through the several volumes of his speeches published a few years ago, one realises that much of the controversy is meaningless. Yet Bhagwat's admission was an important step to remove misconceptions.

On several other issues too, Bhagwat took a refreshingly new and open stand, surprising many within the Sangh as well. His emphatic stand on the Constitution—he even read out the entire Preamble and averred that the RSS has full respect for it, including the words Secularism and Socialism, inserted during the Emergency—and on the status of women are historic from the RSS perspective. Equality and independence—'samaan aur swatantra'—are the words he used to describe the RSS' view on women. He even said that the RSS is ready to accept the proposition that 'all religions are equal'. Many in the RSS hitherto insist that secularism should mean, 'all religions deserve equal respect (*sarva panth samaadar*) and not, 'all religions are equal' (*sarva panth samabhav*).

Some insiders may insist that there is nothing new in what Bhagwat had said and the organisation had always stood for those values. But there always were two parallel streaks in the organisation. An enigma always surrounded its thinking. Bhagwat decided to shatter that enigma.

This is not an easy transition. There is no doubt that Bhagwat has disarmed most critics through his Glasnost. But driving home the new thinking within the rank and file of the organisation, requires no less than a Perestroika—restructuring. Bhagwat's challenge lies in that.

Bhagwat will lead the organisation for many more years to come. He commands enormous respect within the rank and file. With his clarity, candidness and determination, he has the ability to lead the organisation in the direction he wants.

'If not me, who? And if not now, when?' retorted Gorbachev when asked about his reformist zeal. Bhagwat looked equally determined.

25

Leader, Cadre, Parivar

The BJP entered the 39th year of its inception in 2018. The party celebrates 6 April every year as its Foundation Day. The ideological foundation of the party takes it back further by three decades to 1951. In May that year, the Bharatiya Jana Sangh, the ideological progenitor of the BJP, was born.

The face of the Indian polity would have been different had the Congress not transformed itself into a political party in 1947. During the independence struggle, the Congress became a platform for all the disparate political ideologies and groups because of the common objective of securing independence. Once that objective was achieved, different political groups had opted for different political paths to pursue their political goals. Propriety demanded that the Congress dissolved itself post-independence and allowed genuine competitive politics to blossom in India. Even Mahatma Gandhi had recommended that the Congress be disbanded as a political party and developed into Lok Sevak Sangh. The Congress leadership was unwilling to let go of the huge opportunity of presenting themselves before the people of the country as the ones who secured independence and reap the political benefits.

Gandhi died in 1948, while Subhash Chandra Bose had disappeared from the scene in 1945. Thus, there was nobody to challenge this thesis. It proved disadvantageous for the genuine flowering of a functional multi-party democracy in India. The Congress, with the image of 'the party that secured independence,' became the dominant political force, leaving very little space for others to grow.

Thus, when the Bharatiya Jana Sangh was started in 1951, there wasn't much scope in the country's political arena for it to prosper. But then, the Jana Sangh had enjoyed a distinct advantage in the form of its umbilical relationship with the RSS. The RSS, founded by K B Hedgewar in 1925, was essentially a socio-political movement in the initial years until its character was gradually and thoughtfully transformed into that of a socio-cultural organisation by its second chief, M.S. Golwalkar, 'Guruji'. Founded on the premise that the unifying factors of India are its age-old cultural and civilisational markers, the RSS had, in the first two decades, nurtured a constituency with roots in India's cultural and civilisational value system.

The departure of Gandhi had left the Congress in the hands of leaders like Nehru who had no national moorings. They only had the legacy of the freedom struggle. The Communists were expanding their influence in the immediate aftermath of Independence, largely propelled by external developments in the USSR and China. The Jana Sangh became the rallying point for those who believed that India's future was rooted in its own wisdom.

A distinct culture-centric ideology, cadre-based party structure and humility and flexibility in the leadership had led to the Jana Sangh's quick rise in Indian polity. By 1967, its members were in power in a few states through SVD governments and it took another ten years for them to have office at the Centre.

The Jana Sangh's rise also led to the rise of a politics centred on India's own cultural distinctiveness. In the Jana Sangh's scheme of things, India was to be a parliamentary democracy, but with distinct Indian characteristics. 'One Nation; One Culture; One People' became its ideological sheet anchor. Its motto of 'Nation First' had led to the Jana Sangh merging in the Janata Party, while the same motivation led to its re-emergence in 1980 as the Bharatiya Janata Party.

The party has seen highs and lows in the last four decades. But what distinguishes it from other parties is that like the Jana Sangh, the BJP too has grown on the strength of its distinct ideology, cadre-based party structure and political accommodation. Today, it has massively expanded its organisational and political influence. Almost 75 per cent of the country is under its rule with a strong government at the Centre led by Prime Minister Narendra Modi.

Leader, cadre and parivar are the secret of its growth and success. It was the Vajpayee-Advani duo in the past and Modi-Shah in the present who provided able leadership to the party. Well-trained and motivated cadres form the grassroots strength of the party. The sangh parivar, an ideological fraternity of organisations, has always been a strength right from the Jana Sangh days. But the BJP's strength has also been its political parivar—the alliance partners, some of whom have been there as all-weather partners.

In the last few decades, through these distinct advantages, the BJP has risen to occupy the national centrestage of Indian politics. Once condemned as an outcast and regarded as a fringe force, today it dominates every aspect of India's political life. It is closer to its avowed objective of Congress-mukt Bharat. Congress-mukt Bharat is not about exclusivism. It is about achieving what Gandhiji had wanted to achieve in 1948, of bringing in a political culture that has roots in independent India and of promoting healthy political competition based on Indian genius.

As we close in towards that objective, many challenges surmount the party. From 'One nation one people' of the Jana Sangh days to *'Sab ka saath sab ka vikas'* (*Together with all, Development for all*) of Modi, the party stood for the oneness of the nation. Upholding it in a manner that is inclusive is the need of the hour.

26

Ram Mandir Movement
A One-Way Street for BJP

Sometime in the mid-1980s, the then RSS chief Balasaheb Deoras had asked the assembled leaders of the organisation from all the states a simple question: 'Should the RSS plunge fully into the Ram Janmabhoomi movement or allow it to be led by the Vishwa Hindu Parishad and the Ram Janmabhoomi Nyas (the body of saints it had promoted)?' When the assembly unanimously supported the idea of the RSS fully plunging into the movement, Deoras was supposed to have warned them one final time that entering the movement is a one-way street and there won't be any moving back until the goal is achieved.

So when we in the RSS took the decision to join the movement, we knew well that it had to be a movement to the finish. And the finish that we had envisaged was the building of a magnificent Ram temple at the spot, which is described historically as the birthplace of Bhagwan Ram. The decision of the RSS to join the movement has completely transformed the character of it from that of an ostensibly religious one to a movement for national self-respect and honour. The BJP joined the movement subsequently, through its famous Palampur resolution of 1988.

When the movement was launched, we didn't have too many arguments to satisfy the 'eminent intellectuals' of our country and abroad. We were inspired by the simple yet profound desire to see the Ram Mandir come up on the very spot that was believed to be his birthplace. There stood a structure, a non-functional mosque and a functional temple, described as the Babri Masjid. Babar was an invader, and a structure in his name, that too on a spot revered by the people as the birthplace of a legendary figure like Ram, was a sufficient enough reason for millions of ordinary Indians to join the movement. Logic came later; arguments and evidence were developed later. In fact, the most significant arguments in favour of the Ram Mandir were all developed gradually by people who had nothing to do with the RSS or the BJP. On the academic front, foreign scholars like Koenraad Elst, a Belgian, were at the forefront, advancing propositions in the temple's favour. Eminent scholars of Indian origin like Nirad C. Chaudhuri and V.S. Naipaul too lent their support subsequently. But for the majority of ordinary Indians, it was a simple emotional, civilisational appeal—'*Ramlala hum aayenge, mandir vahi banayenge; jahan Ram ka janam hua, mandir wahin banayenge.* (Lord Ram! we will come, we will make the temple there only; on the land that Ram was born on, we will make a temple there only.)'

Nearly three decades later, the one-way road has come to an end. It has crossed many milestones—there were serious efforts to have a negotiated settlement, the controversial structure got demolished and court cases piled up. The future of the Ram temple depended on the verdict and the popular response to it. As a general rule, the nation should wait for the court order and obey it. However, efforts were started by some 'eminent intellectuals' to influence the verdict. A group of them wrote to the Supreme

Court exhorting it to not deliver a verdict in favour of any one community. Almost all of these eminent intellectuals have, at some point, opposed the temple movement. Hence, their sudden activity, pretending to be neutral, caused a lot of suspicion.

It was heartening to see more and more sane voices from among the Muslim community emanating in favour of an amicable settlement. For the larger national society, the Ram temple issue has been more of a question of national honour and dignity. The final judgement in the case was declared by the Supreme Court on 9 November 2019. In accordance with the verdict, the disputed land has been handed over to a trust to build the Ram Janmabhoomi temple.

There was nothing surprising about the BJP, with its strong cultural nationalist credentials, to support the Ram Janmabhoomi (RJB) movement. But the most important political support for the temple movement came in 1989, when the Rajiv Gandhi-led Congress government not only allowed permission for laying the foundation of the temple but also deputed a senior minister, Buta Singh, to personally attend the ceremony.

In the 1989 and 1991 elections, there was a buzz about the RJB movement. But it had more to do with the pseudo-secularism being practised by many parties in the country. One great service that the RJB movement rendered at that time was to generate an intense debate on the country's ethos: 'Cultural nationalism with true secular credentials based on equal respect and non-appeasement' versus 'pseudo secularism with minority appeasement'. The BJP lost elections in the Hindi heartland states like Uttar Pradesh and Madhya Pradesh after the demolition of the controversial structure. Yet, it had succeeded in capturing the public imagination on the crucial question of true secular values.

Having won this battle, the BJP had turned its attention to other important issues before the nation. Ram Janmabhoomi remained the ideological sheet anchor for the larger nationalist movement of which the BJP has been an integral part. However, the party turned its attention to larger governance issues and went on to become the ruling party in 1996, 1998 and 2014. Contrary to the perception of a section of the intelligentsia, the BJP's concept of cultural nationalism represented identity, dignity, freedom and unity. Good governance and development became the mantra of the party. It was this mantra that brought the phenomenon that is Narendra Modi to the forefront.

The tragedy is that the principal opposition party is still stuck in identity politics. Just as Rajiv Gandhi found political virtue in officiating over the shilanyas ceremony in 1989, Rahul Gandhi thinks that temple hopping is the new panacea for all his problems. The Congress's problem is that instead of looking for a Modi, they are trying to bring back a Rajiv Gandhi.

In Ayodhya, the Ram Mandir construction has officially started after the ground-breaking ceremony performed by Prime Minister Narendra Modi on 5 August 2020. The wish of the national society of converting the makeshift temple into a magnificent one will soon be fulfilled. Meanwhile, the country's politics has to focus on the dignity, freedom and unity of this great nation.

27

Somnath to Ayodhya
Journey of an Awakened Civilisation

It was a struggle of five centuries. Hindus never accepted Babur's commander Mir Baqi's vandalism of the temple at the sacred site in Ayodhya, considered the birthplace of Bhagwan Ram. As happened in parts of Europe during the crusades, the site kept changing from temple to mosque to temple. The last time was in 1949 when idols of Ram durbar appeared under the domes of the dysfunctional mosque. Since then it once again became a functioning temple. Another seven decades of wait has finally resulted in the dream of millions of Hindus coming true. The abode of Shri Ram is again springing to life with majesty and magnificence.

It is not a time for chest-thumping or triumphalism. But isn't it time to rejoice? What the Ayodhya movement overcame was not just the opposition of certain Muslim groups, but countless hurdles put up by the courts as well as overzealous secular shenanigans. Not a small thing, given the fact that Hagia Sofia cathedral in Istanbul, in contrast, has been turned once again into a mosque, and Jerusalem is still struggling to decide which history to accept.

Certainly, the construction of the Ram Janmaboomi temple is a glorious epitome of a civilisational reassertion. 'So, new people come up and they begin to look at their world and from being great acceptors, they have become questioners. And I think we should simply try to understand this passion. It is not an ignoble passion at all. It is men trying to understand themselves. Do not dismiss them. Treat them seriously,' warned V.S. Naipaul, the Nobel laureate talking about this reassertion in the mid-1990s.

Renowned British historian Arnold Toynbee had taunted the Hindus four decades before Naipaul commended them. 'Aurangzeb's purpose in building those three mosques (Ayodhya, Kashi and Mathura) was the same intentionally offensive political purpose that moved the Russians to build their Orthodox cathedral in the city centre at Warsaw. Those mosques were intended to signify that an Islamic government was reigning supreme, even over Hinduism's holiest of holy places. Perhaps, the Poles were really kinder in destroying the Russians' self-discrediting monument in Warsaw than you have been in sparing Aurangzeb's mosques,' said Toynbee in a speech at Delhi.

The Orthodox cathedral that Toynbee referred to was Alexander Nevsky Cathedral built by the Russians in the Polish capital Warsaw. When Poland unshackled itself from Czarist Russia after the First World War, the cathedral was demolished by the Polish authorities in the mid-1920s. It took eighteen years to complete the cathedral for the Russians—built between 1894 and 1912, but it didn't survive even fifteen years. Intense debate preceded the demolition. Poles saw it not as a religious monument but as a symbol of Russian domination. Like the pseudo-secularists in India, there were a few voices opposing the demolition, mostly from the Orthodox community. They were contemptuously dismissed as 'Cathedralists'. Not that the Poles were against Orthodox Christianity. There were several other

Orthodox churches in Poland. Many remnants of the Alexander Nevsky Cathedral were later shifted to the Mary Magdalene Orthodox Cathedral in the Warsaw suburb.

Poles took less than ten years after their freedom to remove the Orthodox cathedral. Indians had to wait much longer in the case of Ayodhya. There was a precedent though. The Somnath temple in Gujarat, that was looted and destroyed by Mahmud of Ghazni in 1024, had been restored in 1951 immediately after India's independence. Its restoration had Gandhi's blessings and the initiative came from Sardar Patel and K.M. Munshi. Gandhi's only suggestion to Patel was that the reconstruction of the temple should happen with the funds collected from the people, not from the public exchequer.

Unfortunately, by the time the consecration happened, both Gandhi and Patel were no more. Prime Minister Nehru was opposed to the idea of the reconstruction of the Somnath temple. He first tried to dissuade Munshi. Munshi refused to heed. Nehru then tried to discourage President Rajendra Prasad from attending the consecration ceremony. 'I believe in my religion and cannot cut myself away from it,' Rajendra Prasad bluntly told Nehru. Nehru then wrote to all the chief ministers stating that his government had nothing to do with the Somnath reconstruction and they too shouldn't have anything to do with it.

The Somnath temple returned to its past glory on 11 May 1951, when it was inaugurated in a grand function. Dr Rajendra Prasad was present in person to witness the making of history. 'The Somnath temple signifies that the power of reconstruction is always greater than the power of destruction,' he told in his address, adding 'By rising from its ashes again, this temple of Somnath will proclaim to the world that no man and no power in the world can destroy that for which people have boundless faith and love in their hearts.'

Seventy years after Somnath, the same spirit is bringing Ayodhya to life. Sardar Patel was the prime mover of Somnath reconstruction. But he was not there when it finally happened. Ayodhya owes a lot to Ashok Singhal, but it will miss him on this historic occasion.

When Prime Minister Modi stood at Ayodhya, laying the first brick for the temple, it was a symbolic reiteration of what Dr Rajendra Prasad had said at Somnath almost seventy years ago: 'Today, our attempt is not to rectify history. Our only aim is to proclaim anew our attachment to the faith, convictions and to the values on which our religion has rested since immemorial ages.'

28

Ayodhya is for Ayuddha
Non-War and Peace Communities

Damnatio Memoriae is a Latin phrase roughly meaning 'erasing bad memory'. Although the phrase came into vogue much later, the practice dated back to the Greek and Roman periods in the European history. Erection of statues, not of men of God or of wisdom, but of power was a practice prevalent during those times. At one point, historians point out that there were over 3,000 statues of the emperors in Athens and Rhodes for a population of a few tens of thousands. Then began the practice of Da,mnatio Memoriae, with people demolishing the statues of evil emperors. The practice has returned in the US and Europe again recently.

The Babri story is the Indian equivalent of Damnatio Memoriae. The Babri structure erected by demolishing a flourishing Ram temple at Ayodhya in 1528 by Mughal emperor Babur's commander Mir Baqui was one such bad memory. Iconoclasm was a regular imperial practice during the medieval period for the Semitic religions. The Crusades that the Christians and Muslims fought during the 11th to 14th centuries witnessed large-scale destruction of the sacred places of each other. Thousands of such places still exist in Western European countries. Hagia Sophia, a cathedral of the Byzantine era Constantinople (Istanbul), recently converted into a Mosque by Erdogan's Turkey, is one such living example of the iconoclastic history.

Babur and later Mughal emperors like Aurangzeb were fired by this imperialist iconoclastic zeal and destroyed many prominent Hindu shrines of those times. British historian Arnold Toynbee described these destructions as the product of an 'intentionally offensive political purpose'. Toynbee, delivering Maulana Azad Memorial Lecture hosted by the ICCR in Delhi in 1960, referred to the Alexander Nevsky Cathedral built in 1893 by the Russians in Warsaw.

'By its very presence, the Russian Orthodox Church declares to the world that in the western terrains along the Vistula, mighty Orthodox rule has taken root,' wrote Tsar Alexander III's chancellery about the construction of that Cathedral. As discussed earlier, when the Poles got out of the Tsar rule after the First World War, they promptly demolished the cathedral in 1924 calling the structure not as a religious monument but as a symbol of Russian occupation. Toynbee equated mosques in Ayodhya, Mathura and Kashi with the cathedral in Warsaw and taunted Indians that 'the Poles were really kinder in destroying the Russians' self-discrediting monument in Warsaw than you have been sparing Aurangzeb's mosques.'

Three decades after Toynbee's taunt, the Babri structure went down and the first brick was laid for the restoration of a magnificent temple after another three decades. The larger national consensus over Ayodhya, like the one witnessed after the revocation of Article 370 in Jammu and Kashmir, can't be missed. There were some questions, but only about 'how' they were done, not about 'why' they were done.

Some still talk about converting the upcoming temple at Ayodhya into a Mosque at an unknown future date 'on the lines of Hagia Sophia', and a few crassly communal leaders still claim that '*Babri masjid thi, hai aur rahegi*', (It was, is and will be a Babri mosque). But they don't represent the larger Muslim community which understands and appreciates that the issue was not worth losing time and lives any more.

Ideally, a solution based on mutual agreement would have been the best climax for the issue. Efforts made in that direction in early 1990s during Chandrasekhar's and Narasimha Rao's regimes did not yield any results. Thankfully, that larger consensus is discernible now. Ever since the Supreme Court judgment came, both communities displayed maturity and positivity towards the issue. There was no chest thumping or triumphalism from the Hindu side, while there wasn't any unwholesome reaction from the Muslim side either.

Ram and Ayodhya are greatest unifiers of India. Ram Manohar Lohia, the renowned socialist leader of the last century, used to say that Ram, Krishna and Shiv signify India's civilisational identity. 'You just stand outside a temple in Rameswaram in the South or Badrinath in the North; you will find Hindustan there,' he used to say. Ayodhya is a sacred place for Hindus, Buddhists, Sikhs and Jains. Ram is revered for his supreme human qualities by millions of others irrespective of religion. The only message that Ayodhya emanates is about that larger unity and goodwill among the people.

'You will find Ram in different forms in different Ramayanas; but Ram is present everywhere; Ram is for all. That is why Ram is the connecting link in India's unity in diversity', said Prime Minister Modi at the recent Bhumi Puja event at Ayodhya.

Swami Chinmayananda, founder of the Chinmaya Mission gave a unique definition to Ayodhya. He was one of the pillars of the movement until his demise in 1993. 'Ayodhya, the word itself means 'Ayuddha', that is, non-war or peace. It is for Ayuddha (no conflict) that we are fighting. Just as the World War was for peace, we are no doubt fighting, but only for establishing peace and progress in our country,' he used to say. The temple at Ayodhya should pave the way for Ayuddha—peace forever among communities.

29

In Sita's Footsteps

Whereas the country has celebrated Ram Navami, the birth anniversary of Ram in the first week of April, one region spread across India and Nepal—Mithilanchal—prefers to celebrate Sita Navami, the birth anniversary of Sita. She is the divine consort of Ram for the world, but for the people of Mithilanchal, she is their daughter, sister, and simply put, their girl. They call her Kishori, or a youthful girl. The people of Mithila, the Maithils, have on one hand, great pride over their 'Kishori', Sita or Janki, but on the other hand, they carry great pain in their hearts for all the sufferings that their 'Kishori' had to endure through Ayodhya to Lanka and back. So much so that although Sita belonged to Mithilanchal, they hesitate to name their girls after her, not necessarily out of any superstition, but out of a sentiment for Sita's lifetime of sufferings.

Unfortunately, it became the universal portrayal of not only Sita, but women in general in India. They are projected as *'abala'*— feeble, born to suffer. Sita epitomised those sufferings. This kind of portrayal of women as weak and destined for suffering and submission is of medieval origin. Several writings of the medieval period suffer from this anomalous portrayal of women as weak and needful of protection from men.

Medieval Europe had people running around offering lineage to Adam, God's original human creation, for a price. Men continued to enjoy supremacy while women were being burnt alive as witches. There were ludicrous debates over whether women should be treated as humans or not. Not until the early 20th century did women in the West get voting rights. Even at the dawn of the 21st century, several church denominations were undecided over whether to allow women at the pulpit or not. They cite St Paul's dictum in 1 Timothy 2:12 ('I do not permit a woman to teach or to have authority over a man') as a universal injunction to deny women the right to stand at the pulpit. The feminist movements of the West have been a product of this oppressive situation that prevailed in parts of the world.

But the history of India's womanhood fascinates even the most modern feminists. Medieval distortions apart, Indian understanding of womanhood has been that of equality, divinity, self-respect and self-assertion. Sita epitomises not weakness or meekness, but these qualities. In fact, her very name Sita can be expanded to highlight her qualities—Strong, Intelligent, Transparent, Assertive.

To understand the personality of Sita, one has to turn to the original author of the epic Ramayana, Valmiki. Sita's portrayal in Valmiki's Ramayana was that of a woman of courage, wisdom and knowledge, self-esteem and astuteness. She was discarded by parents, and found by King Janak in an agrarian field. She was raised as a Kshatriya woman and married into a noble Kshatriya family of Dasharath. She was kidnapped by Raavan, rescued by her husband Ram, only to be rejected again. She was sheltered and nursed by the sage Valmiki in forests and rejoined Mother Earth.

To understand this journey of Sita, the best source, other than the original Valmiki's Ramayan, is the series of lectures delivered by acclaimed scholar-politician Rt. Hon. V.S. Srinivasa Sastri. His *Lectures on the Ramayana* is a fascinating read; more importantly, the three lectures on Sita.

Sita comes out as an extremely adorable and strong-willed woman in Srinivasa Sastri's narration. Sita was in a way singularly responsible for the war between Ram and Raavan. 'I had a dream,' she declares to Anasuya, that 'I would lead my life in forests.' And she had decided that to be her destiny. When Ram persuades her to stay back in the palace during his fourteen-year sojourn to forests—the *Vanvas*—Sita fiercely resists the idea, almost castigating Ram of trying to get rid of her. 'I am a Kshatriya girl. I won't go under the control of other people, be it Kaikeyi or Bharat,' she declares firmly. Ram admits that Sita was a courageous woman. 'You wonder why I said "no" at first? I didn't know what a courageous woman you really were. I thought you might be like ordinary women. Now I see who you are and what you are,' he says. Together, they leave for the *Vanvas*—with Lakshman following them.

Sita didn't lose this courage throughout her life. Even in the face of unbearable hardships in Raavan's court, Sita remained steadfast, not losing her courage and composure. Some narratives portray Sita as a disheartened and weeping creature in Ashoka Van—the pine forest in which Raavan had kept her. Ashoka Van was described by zealous writers as Shoka Van—garden of sorrow. But the original narrative goes differently. Sita did suffer, probably cried, but her courage didn't diminish. She withstood all hardships. And when Raavan came to finally persuade her to accept his proposal for marriage, Sita refused to look at him; instead, she held up a blade of grass and addressed Raavan through that. 'I have so much power in me that if only I care to direct it against you, you would be a mass of ash. But I refrain from doing so because I want to preserve my Tapas—divine power. Besides, I have not received an order from Ram to defend myself. The burden rests upon him, and he himself should come and save me,' she thundered.

Here, Sita was reminding Ram of his Dharma as a Kshatriya and also as a husband. There were occasions when Sita would engage in a discourse of Dharma with Ram. She even taunts Ram for his eagerness to go to the rescue of the sages who were suffering at the hands of the rakshasas. 'When a Kshatriya, trained to fight, finds his weapons ready, or when agni—the fire—finds fuel near, then there is danger. It provokes him to an exhibition of strength,' she warns. It could as well be a universal lesson for all countries. This shows the knowledge and wisdom of Sita. When Hanuman wanted to punish the women guards at Ashoka Van after Raavan's death, Sita prevented him saying they were not the cause of her misery as they were only obeying the orders of their master. Then come her jewels of wisdom on non-harming and non-retaliation. 'The righteous man ought not to be turned from the right by the sin of the sinner. The rule of honour is inviolable. Good men have only one jewel, their unblemished conduct, and they must guard it, come what may. Be they good men or bad, be they deserving of death, still must they be pardoned and treated with mercy by one claiming to be an Aryan. For, no one is above error,' she tells Hanuman.

Sita's courage, coupled with her wisdom, manifested in her self-respect and self-confidence. In fact, the portrayal of Sita and Draupadi in our epics indicates the respect and honour that Indian society has accorded to women's self-esteem. Sita was submissive only to the extent that her self-honour was not violated, whether the violator was Raavan or Ram. Ram raises questions over her fidelity not once, but twice. The first occasion was after the defeat and death of Raavan. Sita was aghast. 'You are not a lowly man, nor am I a lowly woman,' she chides him. Her hurt self-respect comes out in her words. 'You have let your ill-temper run away with your judgment, and like a low-bred man, esteemed me lightly as though I was no better than the ordinary type of woman,' she accuses him. 'Only in name am I of Janaka's family. I came out of the pure ploughed earth,' she thunders. Agni, the fire God, stands testimony to Sita's purity, refusing to touch her. Thus she comes out of Ram's first fidelity test, but not without warning him about his lack of wisdom.

This courageous self-assertion of Sita can be seen again and again in Ramayana. The second time when Ram wanted her to leave was immediately after the return to the throne in Ayodhya. This time, the excuse was that the citizens had suspicions about her. Sita was pregnant at that time. Ram couldn't muster courage to ask her to leave. It falls upon Lakshman, who takes her in a chariot to the banks of river Ganges and conveys the decision of the King. Lakshman was heartbroken, but Sita was stunned, yet composed. She asks Lakshman to convey to Ram that she would live until she gives birth to the children and prove her chastity.

Sita was given shelter and protection by Valmiki in his ashram in the forests. Sita gave birth to Luv and Kush, the twins. She raised them as warriors, taught them archery and other war skills. She would personally guide and supervise their military training as there was nobody else to do the same in the forests. During the course of a yagna that Ram conducted, the horse enters the forest where they were all dwelling. Sita's twins withhold the horse, war ensues and Ram's army is roundly defeated. Ram comes to the hermitage and realises that the children were his own. He wants Sita back. Here again, Sita comes out as a woman of high self-esteem. 'This earth is not for me,' she tells Ram, and categorically adds, 'neither this husband, nor the subjects whom no proof can ever convince.' She seeks for Mother Earth to open up and rejoins her.

This was quintessential Sita, a brave, determined, wise and self-respecting woman. This is the Indian womanhood that our ancestors had idolised. For their stubbornness, neither Sita nor Draupadi were decried; instead, they were given a place of honour as great women.

Historically, in our civilisation, women are respected for their wisdom, self-respect and dignity. The world's most ancient literature, the Vedas, contain a number of verses written by women scholars and saints. Gargi, Maitreyi, Lopamudra were some of them. There were at least thirty women authors of the Vedic hymns. The famous dialogue that Gargi had with Yagnavalkya, over the nature of *Brahmaan* is a tribute to the scholarship of that great Vedic philosopher and also a testimony to the enormous respect that women enjoyed in the Vedic period.

A similar incident happened much later when Adi Shankara and Mandana Mishra engaged in a *Shastraartha*—scholarly dialogue. When Mandana Mishra fails, his wife Ubhaya Bharati, jumps in to challenge Adi Shankara. Shankara was forced to return to his studies before coming back to face Ubhaya Bharati.

This should be the essence of true feminism. Geena D. Andersen, the renowned Australian feminist, puts it succinctly, 'Feminism is not about making women stronger. It is about changing the way the world perceives their strength.' We need to teach our generation to respect the strength and glory of womanhood. What better occasion than Sita Jayanti for that!

30

Despite the People

'The best lack all conviction, while the worst are full of passionate intensity.' In his 1921 classic poem 'The Second Coming', W.B. Yeats talks about the failure of the system, leading to anarchy all around. 'Things fall apart, the centre cannot hold/ Mere anarchy is loosed upon the world/ the blood-dimmed tide is loosed, and everywhere/ the ceremony of innocence is drowned,' he laments.

An anarchy let loose by the forces of the state itself, people as mere innocent bystanders often subjected to repression and violence for the sin of believing in traditions and having convictions—this is Kerala today, courtesy the false zeal of the non-believing Marxist government, which forced a change in the temple tradition that nobody seemed to support.

The Marxist government of Kerala is unleashing harsh measures against the Ayyappa devotees who are peacefully protesting. The protesters include thousands of women. Hundreds of devotees have been arrested by the state government and hundreds more harassed on the streets, allegedly by the CPM cadres. All this in the name of implementing the Supreme Court order of letting women into the Sabarimala temple.

In Sabarimala, there is a tradition that women between the ages of ten and fifty do not enter the shrine. What are the origins of this tradition? There are several versions and stories that answer this question, but no devotee in Kerala or elsewhere has ever objected to the practice.

It is believed that the God in Sabarimala, Lord Ayyappa, had given a commitment to Goddess Malikapurathamma, from a shrine nearby that he would one day accept her proposal to marry when the first-time 'kanni' swamis stop visiting his temple, and the Goddess is waiting in a nearby temple for that to happen. But that hasn't happened yet, as thousands of first-time swamis continue to visit the shrine, prolonging the Goddess's wait. Following in her footsteps, women in the age group of ten to fifty years refrain from entering Ayyappa's abode at Sabarimala.

Such traditions exist in all places, among all religions. They may sometimes look strange or out of place to outsiders. Some may want the old traditions to go. But then, unless the said traditions come in the way of public order and morality, the reform should be left to the practitioners themselves. Opposition to this harmless tradition came not from any true devotee, but from those who explicitly proclaimed that they were non-believers and, hence, had nothing to do with that tradition directly. Their argument was that the tradition is against gender equality and hence regressive. They also hurled insinuations that the temple tradition treats women shabbily by calling them impure during the menstrual cycle.

What offended the people of Kerala the most are these nonsensical arguments. Kerala has innumerable temples, churches and mosques. It is a state with a rich tradition and practice of religiosity. The women of Kerala are the most religious and lead the way in following religious customs and practices. What infuriated them the most was the insinuation that there was gender inequality in Kerala and, by extension, injustice is being done to women.

Kerala is the only state, besides the Khasis in Meghalaya, that follows a matriarchal system. Women dominate family and social life in Kerala. Teaching them about gender equality is like carrying coal to Newcastle. But then, the over-zealous crusaders have little concern for the reality on the ground. That is what irks the people of Kerala—men and women alike—the most. Today, both men and women in equal numbers are on the streets protesting the efforts of the Kerala government to push women into the Sabarimala temple forcefully.

It is true that Article 14 to 21 of the Indian Constitution provide for certain fundamental rights of which the Right to Equality is among the most important. But these rights are personal in nature. In a similar vein, Article 25 to 30 provide certain rights to religious institutions too. Article 25 and 26 talk about the Hindu religious institutions having the right to manage their affairs according to their customs and traditions. These rights too need to be kept in mind unless it is explicitly proven that they are in contravention of fundamental rights in a particular context.

In any political system, there is an unwritten agreement between the people and their government that each takes care of the other. The governor and the governed in a democracy are in a direct contract. But of late, we are witnessing a new phenomenon. Former British diplomat, Carne Ross, so eloquently writes about this phenomenon in his book *The Leaderless Revolution: A growing number of political actors* 'who are neither politicians nor conventional political parties, nor accountable to anyone but themselves' are wielding enormous influence in policy-making these days.

Talking about those actors he says: 'Such groups also contribute to a growing and unpleasant extremism in political debate. Adept at a one-sided presentation of the evidence, these groups advocate black-and-white positions with aggressive vigour and armfuls of one-sided research—often representing those who oppose them as foolish and sometimes evil. Facts and reasoned analysis are invariably the victims.'

This is precisely what is happening in Sabarimala debate. The ordinary people, the governed, are hapless as the political, media and NGO establishment in Kerala is pitted against them. Our politics and policy-making have been hijacked by middlemen representing various group interests.

It is nobody's case to argue that traditions can't change. The Kerala society has shown enormous resilience in this matter. With the motivation provided by Mahatma Gandhi, the then Maharaja of Travancore, together with many eminent people was at the forefront in the 1940s of opening the temples to all sections of Kerala society. Any reform, unless urgently required to be imposed from the top, should be encouraged to come from within. Else, we will be hastening the process of the 'leaderless revolution', where 'ordinary people will take power and change politics', as Ross puts it.

31

After Empowerment, Freedom and Dignity

The problem with some policies is that they are at least a decade behind the thoughts and aspirations of the people. Unless we address this mismatch, seemingly noble policies also fail to do justice to the targeted sections of the population.

Take, for example, the aspirations of sections like SCs, STs and women. Today, the aspiration of the downtrodden is not just about power-sharing but a share in decision-making. Through various policies we have addressed the issue of power-sharing. But did it lead to them reaching decision-making positions?

Similarly, about women, the discourse fashionable today is about empowerment. What does empowerment mean? We assume that the aspiration or desire among the women is for positions on par with men. Our policies are structured in that direction. We hardly realise that while it is fashionable to showcase these things as our commitment to women's empowerment, the aspirational discourse has gone much farther.

The urge and aspiration among the women today is for dignity and freedom. Any further talk of empowering women will be seen as condescension because empowerment is today seen as entitlement. We need to rise to the current sentiment—of empowerment with dignity and honour.

Women are in commanding positions in many areas of private and public life in our country. Even in rural India, women are greatly empowered through their presence and positions outside the four walls of their homes. Initially, this change needed support and prodding but now it is on an auto mode.

Yet, the challenge of dignity and freedom remains. The empowerment that we talk about has certainly given them positions, but not necessarily the dignity and freedom that they deserve. Social media is a good test case, since it is a truly democratic media. It reflects human behaviour through an unadulterated, unedited prism. It is here that one comes across extreme forms of deprecating behaviour with respect to women. In varied degrees, this prevails in all walks of life.

Our laws, societal norms and customs need to be looked at from this new reality. There was a time when women needed protection. We built laws and institutions keeping that need in mind. It was felt later that women needed empowerment. We addressed that need too. But today's need is to revisit our polity to accord dignity and freedom to our womenfolk.

Mahatma Gandhi used to say that real independence would be when a woman in this country can walk around on the streets alone at midnight. An easy way to think of this would be from a security perspective. But another interpretation could be about dignity. How does society look at a lone woman roaming the streets at midnight? Just like how it looks at a man in similar circumstances or with suspicion, if not disdain? Does she enjoy freedom of choice or is she branded promiscuous?

This brings up the crux of the issue. Can a woman be respected just as a woman, without any strings attached? Or she will be respected only when she is a 'mother' or 'sister'? Is her freedom and self-expression equal to that of a man?

There is an instructive anecdote in the Shanti Parva in Mahabharata. Yudhishtir, having won the war, approaches Bhishma, who is on the bed of arrows awaiting death, seeking advise on statecraft. Draupadi, the feisty princess, was passing by, and laughs out loud. Yudhishtir remonstrates; but Bhishma stops him and submits that Draupadi's laughter was valid. 'In a full House, when she was being disrobed, I remained a mute witness. Am I today qualified to teach you Raj Dharma? That is what Draupadi's laughter meant,' says Bhishma.

The Indian approach to womanhood is replete with messages that accord dignity and freedom to women, not just a higher pedestal. Manu is criticised for talking about the duty of the society to protect women. But Manu also grants women the right to divorce under four different circumstances.

Women face two extremes in our society. At one end is the vulgarity of objectification. The higher a woman rises the greater the objectification becomes. How they appear, how they dress and how they style their hair or wear their footwear becomes the subject. What follows is violence, both physical and emotional.

But the other extreme is equally demeaning. In the name of security, we deny women their natural choices and freedom. Ideally, we should be allowing greater intermixing of both sexes. But regressive beliefs at one level and questions of safety at another encourage us towards greater segregation. This gender-based segregation starts at the school level itself and continues.

This goes to ridiculous extents like every instance of boys and girls coming together being seen as sinful. Within accepted societal norms, allowing greater intermixing of boys and girls will actually help develop a healthy attitude of friendship and mutual respect.

It is time we turned our attention towards this question of dignity and freedom. Laws for women's protection are important, but not enough. We also need to revisit our customs like marriage, family and divorce. What should be the marriageable age, what should be the procedure and what if the marriage doesn't work—all these aspects need a fresh look through the prism of dignity and freedom, not just through an abstract idea of 'family honour'.

Nobody wants families to collapse or promiscuity to pervade. We have seen the ill-effects of the collapsing family system in Western societies. But smugness shouldn't be our way. Just because the Western models are flawed doesn't automatically mean ours are perfect. A vibrant society should have the courage for continuous reform. Unchanging eternal values, and ever-changing social order is what Indian wisdom stands for.

Remember Tennyson: 'The old order changeth yielding place to new; And God fulfils himself in many ways; Lest one good custom should corrupt the world.'

32

Because India Comes First

The BJP started its journey three decades ago with the slogan of 'United India-Strong India'. The challenge came from not just the divisive politics of caste and religion but also a formidable section of the intelligentsia. It is the journey of that idea of India that culminated in the historic victory yesterday, in the process decimating the politics of caste, religion and vote banks. That idea has become pan-Indian, encompassing all regions and sections of society. That is the central message of 2014 election, and therein lies the future of India.

Starting with just two seats in 1984, the BJP rose quickly to become the ruling party by 1996. There was no looking back after that. Thirty years after its first election, the party registered a thumping victory in 2014. Undoubtedly, the credit goes to Narendra Modi. He turned that election into a quasi-presidential one. He travelled to every nook and corner of the country, addressed thousands of meetings and occupied many hours of airtime. In the process, he set a new benchmark in politics that might be difficult for any future leader to meet.

In Modi and the BJP, the people of this country have seen not only an alternative government to the disastrous one headed by the Congress, but an alternative vision, too. It is that vision that sets Modi apart. He has an economic vision that cares for the last man—the proverbial chaiwala. It is this vision that has brought millions of India's poor to him, deserting their traditional caste-based parties.

He has a much-discussed social vision. He views India as one, above the differences of caste, religion and region. 'Justice for all and appeasement of none'—the traditional conviction of the BJP marks Modi's social vision, which seems to have attracted large sections of the minorities. Above all, Modi's clean and efficient governance model, as against the dynastic, corrupt and inefficient one provided by the Congress, appears to be the game-changer.

Modi is driven by the passion to make India strong. India needs a strong economy that caters to the last man by invoking the mantra of development and growth. It should strengthen the hands of the poor by facilitating more employment. It shouldn't turn them into perpetual beggars, surviving at the mercy of the government-offered doles. For that, our infrastructure has to improve quickly. India's security, both external and internal, needs greater attention. We have to pay special attention to strengthening our border infrastructure.

Most importantly, we need to address the serious problem of corruption and mal-governance. Corruption is eating into the vitals of our nation, killing our efficiency; it is leading to severe social unrest, violence and breeding insurgencies. There is also a need to strengthen our social fabric. We need a government that treats all people as equals and doesn't discriminate on the basis of their religion or region. It should be benevolent to all and tyrannical to none. No one, minority or majority, should feel discrimination or apprehension.

This is a tall order. It requires great leadership qualities, like clarity of vision, courage of conviction, will power, selflessness and team spirit. In Modi, the people of India have perhaps seen all those qualities. With great hope and anticipation, they voted him to power.

The RSS cadres have worked tirelessly with two specific mandates; one, to reach out to the people and inform them of the challenges the country is facing today and the need for a change in government to overcome them; and two, to encourage more people to use their franchise. It gives us immense satisfaction that there has been remarkable success on both counts. People have voted for good government and in the process, polling percentages too have gone up in different parts of the country.

With a sense of contentment, we return to our core activity outside the political arena, of character-building and social service. We have complete trust and faith in the present leadership to take appropriate decisions in governance matters. The RSS doesn't interfere in those matters.

FACING THE FACTS

'To understand current and future conflict, cultural rifts must be understood, and culture rather than the State must be accepted as the reason for war. Thus, Western nations will lose predominance if they fail to recognise the irreconcilable nature of cultural tensions.'

—Samuel Huntington

33

Liberal Fascists

It is an old technique of our pseudo-intellectuals to attack and abuse, but never engage in a debate or discussion over the issues raised or the arguments made. *Sesham Kopena Poorayet*—goes an old adage. What remains when you run out of arguments is anger and abuse.

What Dr Subramanian Swamy had written in an article titled 'How to wipe out Islamic terror in India' were his views. One may or may not agree with his views. The article was found fit for publication by the editor of a prestigious Mumbai-based English daily.

Ideally, our intellectuals should have responded by countering Dr Swamy's arguments and opinions. Instead what we heard were endless invectives. I am not giving any opinion on the content of the article here. But how can I or anybody else deny Dr Swamy his right to articulate his views?

In fact, the political mission of many Islamists is under scrutiny all over the world. Tons of literature can be found in the US and Europe over political Islam. In most liberal parts of the world, issues relating to Islam and its political ambitions are debated and opinions are expressed freely. But in our country, it is a complete taboo.

I am not surprised about the reactions from politicians like Digvijay Singh. In fact, we can ignore them. For they are just merchants of votes, rather unscrupulous. They don't read books that they go to release. We don't need to imagine that they had read Dr Swamy's piece before condemning him. They are knowledge-proof and information-proof. All that they know is to cynically exploit every opportunity for their narrow vote-bank politics. In fact, they must be cribbing and wallowing that 'Osamaji' had not phoned them before getting killed so that they could have declared a grand nexus between the CIA and the RSS in eliminating 'Osamaji'—'part of a global anti-Muslim conspiracy'. Ignore them.

But what about our intellectual brigade that churned out choicest sobriquets at Dr Swamy for daring to write that article? What about our Minority Commission which was 'seriously considering' taking legal action against him?

Don't forget these were the very same people who vigorously defended M.F. Hussain, using their full vocal might, when he painted Durga Mata, Sita Mata and Bharat Mata in the nude. That was described as 'artistic freedom'. And these were the ones who were defending seditious bellows of Arundhati Roy, S.A.R. Geelani and others. That was freedom of expression. Why then can Dr Swamy not enjoy that freedom?

But that is how our pseudo intellectuals operate. They did it before too, several times, and with several others. When Syed Shahabuddin was attacking Justice Krishna Aiyer on the Shah Bano judgment or when he was haranguing against Salman Rushdie—remember, without even reading the book *Satanic Verses*—these intellectuals were not seen anywhere to stop him. They were mute spectators to the fundamentalist

Muslims' targeting of Taslima Nasreen and their hurling of choicest invectives at her. Even to this day, she runs from pillar to post every six months to ensure that the Indian Government doesn't throw her out under the pressure exerted by the fundamentalist groups.

In all these cases, the refrain of these pseudo intellectuals is that the sentiments and sensitivities of the Muslims must be kept in mind. Let me recall that when Ayatollah Khomeini declared fatwa of death against Rushdie, the great American Democrat and former President Jimmy Carter didn't ask for the Ayatollah or the Muslims to show greater sensitivity to the right to freedom of expression of other people. Instead, he only called for greater Western sensitivity to Muslim feelings. So did Margaret Thatcher of the UK.

Our pseudo intellectuals don't bother when a Derek van Gogh is murdered or a Geert Wilders is made to make umpteen number of rounds of the courts or a Scandinavian magazine office becomes a target of repeated attacks for an ordinary cartoon depicting the Prophet or an Ayan Hirsi Ali is hounded out of Netherlands. Their freedom of expression doesn't count. They pounce on Dr Swamy in the same manner for using a platform to express his views. He must be thrown out of Harvard; he must be prosecuted. Now, are they not the real Fascists—the Liberal Fascists?

34

Know Your Terrorist

We all admire the spirit of Mumbai. But we forget the fact that several other cities too experienced similar attacks in the last few decades. Pune, Ahmedabad, Hyderabad, Jaipur, Delhi, Varanasi—many cities and many incidents. What is common about most of these incidents is that the investigations have proceeded nowhere. Except in the cases of the Parliament attack and 26/11 Mumbai attacks, the investigating agencies could hardly achieve any breakthrough in the investigations in the other cases of terrorism.

All that we hear from those who are responsible is helplessness and despair. Former Home Minister Chidambaram's statement that there was no intelligence failure perplexed everybody in the world. On one hand, he admitted that there was no prior intelligence input about the impending attack, yet he is not willing to accept that there is some failure.

There was no security failure either. All that the former chief minister of Maharashtra was ready to bemoan about was that the Home Ministry was not in his control. The Mumbai ATS Chief would appear on TV the whole day but only to tell people that they were still clueless about the perpetrators.

No wonder the ruling party politicians become apologists and the opposition, the attackers. Apologists would reassure you that 'behind each success of the terrorists there were ninety-nine successes of the security agencies which go unsung'. What are those 'ninety-nine unsung successes' of the agencies? There was not a single terrorist attack in the US after the 9/11. The entire world knew that the US is 'enemy number one' for the jihadists. It is also a fact that there were numerous attempts by the terrorists to attack on the US. But the US had been successful in thwarting the Jihadi attempts so far. One incident was when a rogue Pakistani parked his car near the Times Square and attempted to detonate it. Another rogue Pakistani hatched a huge conspiracy in 2009 to blow up a number of US-bound planes from London. But the British agencies could not only prevent that disaster but arrest the entire gang of terrorists too.

Our ignoramus leaders would then try another argument. 'Oh, the Americans are attacked in Iraq and Afghanistan regularly,' they say. Pity that they don't understand the difference between a war and civilian terror. Also, they want to compare India with Afghanistan and Iraq. Thank God, they are not our rulers yet. They will certainly bring India to that brink if allowed to become one.

Then come the irresponsible ones. It is better to ignore them. In 2006, Congress leader Arjun Singh kicked up a storm in his own party's teacup when he blamed the Mumbai terror attacks on the RSS in a cabinet meeting chaired by the then Prime Minister Manmohan Singh.

There is one worrisome lot though, whose writings and statements, knowingly or otherwise cause some concern. This lot includes strategic experts, men in the agencies and column writers. Several of them have started declaring that India has entered the age of what they call as 'indigenous jihad' or 'domestic/homegrown terrorism'. Is this true? Is the phenomenon of Indian Mujahideen the reason enough to conclude so? If the local support to the acts of terror perpetrated from across the border is what we are describing as the homegrown terror, then it has always existed. But if we were to presume that terrorism in the hinterland in India is a product of the domestic network only, we would probably be walking into a well-laid-out trap by the perpetrators in our neighbourhood.

This raises the serious question of why we lack full understanding of the nature of terror in India. While the world outside is into full-blown action in dismantling this terror network, we, the worst victims of terror according to the US National Counter Terrorism Center in Washington, D.C., are still debating as to what form of terror it is; whether it is homegrown or externally sponsored.

Herein lies the greatest failure of our security establishment in general and the former Home Minister P. Chidambaram in particular. The direction in which he conducted the Internal Security apparatus only culminated in confusion among the agencies, demoralisation or marginalisation of the Law and Order machinery in the states and creation of agencies like the NIA which lacked knowhow or 'know-why' and was yet entrusted with tasks that they are ill-equipped to handle. It is not enough to pump in money in the name of police modernisation; the Home Ministry needed vision, which the previous incumbent seemed to be lacking.

The result was we were in utter confusion with regard to the very identity of the perpetrators of these crimes. There is SIMI; there is Indian Mujahadeen; and then there surfaced another gang called the 'Deccan Mujahadin' at the time of the Mumbai blasts of 2006. Are they really homegrown? This phenomenon of using loosely organised groups with fictitious identities has started long ago. Any good intelligence officer would say that this will be textbook tactic of an insurgent group; to create an impression that terrorism is homegrown; if possible to create terror modules in which not just the Muslims but even the Hindus would be members. Richard Headly is a test in case. A Pakistani who was born in the US and acquired complete American identity including a name, Headley turned out to be working for the ISI. Can we rule out the possibility in the case of the IM or SIMI or other organisations?

Problem with these outfits is that they are quite amorphous. Even after almost a decade nobody knew fully what this IM is all about. Interrogation of the SIMI cadres revealed that it essentially branched out of SIMI. SIMI is mandated to undertake selective killings while the IM will indulge in mass killings through terrorism. Riaz Bhatkal, Md Tauqeer, Md Faisal and Amir Raza Khan are some of the names associated with this outfit. But nobody has any clue as to what the hierarchy is.

For those who talk about the homegrown terror, it must be remembered that almost all of these leaders are suspected to be either in Pakistan or in safe havens arranged by ISI elsewhere, like Dubai and Nepal. Most of the IM operatives come from one school in Azamgarh. They have active liaison with LeT, JiM and HUJI.

Our agencies groped in dark due to lack of intelligence and knowledge about these outfits. And for self-seeking leaders, this confusion remained an opportunity to indulge in petty politicking.

There was ineptness—in identifying the perpetrators, in bringing them to book through strict laws, in punishing them, and most importantly in implementing that punishment.

As eminent writer Brahma Chellany commented in an article: 'The ugly truth is that transnational terrorists see India as an easy target because it imposes no costs on them and their patrons.'

35

Citizenship Act
For Persecuted Minorities

The Convention Relating to the Status of Refugees, also known as the 1951 Refugee Convention, is described as the Magna Carta of refugee rights. Under this Convention, a comprehensive charter of the rights of the refugees was developed. These rights are quite elaborate and include freedom of religion, employment, housing and wage earning, right to own movable and immovable assets, right to public education, social justice, access to legal remedies, right to travel documents, and even an important right to cease to be a refugee by seeking citizenship of the host country.

The Indian government, in its own wisdom, had decided not to become a signatory to this convention during the early years of independence. As a result, the United Nations High Commissioner on Refugees (UNHCR) didn't have any jurisdiction over India until 1981. That year, the Indian government allowed partial functioning of the UNHCR in the country by granting temporary residence permits for its officials. India does have a problem of refugees, but it has, in all these decades, dealt with that problem through its own legal instruments or through bilateral treaties. When some refugees enter India with UNHCR refugee identity cards, India, although not a signatory, has shown lenience towards them as well as asylum-seekers.

Since India is not guided by this international convention, it has, from time to time, promulgated different executive orders and laws to deal with the problem of refugees. Latest among such acts was the Citizenship Amendment Act (CAA) 2019. The CAA 2019 deals with a historical problem of immigration that had roots in India's partition. India was divided on religious lines at the time of its independence, leading to a large-scale migration of minorities across both sides. An estimated fifteen million people had crossed over to either side of the newly created borders. In order to address this migration and ensuing human suffering, the then Prime Ministers of India and Pakistan, Jawaharlal Nehru and Liaquat Ali Khan, respectively, had signed an agreement, famously called Nehru–Liaquat Pact. Both the Prime Ministers had agreed to take care of the interests of the minorities in their respective countries. India became a vibrant secular democracy. Today, it can boast of hosting various religious minorities enjoying equal rights under its Constitution.

Unfortunately, in Pakistan, soon after the Pact, things went awry. Liaquat Ali Khan was assassinated in 1951 and Khwaza Nazimuddin became the second Prime Minister there. Nazimuddin had demonstrated scant respect for Jinnah's or Liaquat Ali's secular commitments. In his book *The Ahmadis and the Politics of Religious Exclusion in Pakistan*, Ali Usman Qasmi quotes Nazimuddin as declaring, 'I do not agree that religion is a private affair nor do I agree that in an Islamic state every citizen has identical rights, no matter what his caste, creed or faith be.' The very first constitution, adopted by Pakistan's National Assembly in 1956, had declared Pakistan to be an Islamic

Republic. Minorities in Pakistan started facing trouble and began to migrate to India, both from East and West Pakistan.

By the mid 1960s, tensions started mounting between the East and West wings of Pakistan because of ethnic and linguistic reasons, finally resulting in the division of Pakistan and creation of Bangladesh in 1971. Brutal repression that preceded the creation of Bangladesh had led to another major wave of migration of minorities from East Pakistan into India, largely into states such as West Bengal, Assam and Tripura. While the official figures put the number of refugees to India during the period at 1.2 million, unofficial figures go up to 10 million.

Bangladesh was created not on religious, but ethnic-linguistic identity. Under its first Prime Minister Sheikh Mujibur Rahman, it emerged as a secular country. Prime Ministers of India and Bangladesh, Indira Gandhi and Rahman, respectively, signed a 12-point agreement in 1972. It premised on the assurance that minorities in Bangladesh will be taken care of by the new regime there while the Indian government will accommodate those who had migrated into India. Sadly, Bangladesh too followed Pakistan's trajectory soon. Ziaur Rahman captured power in Bangladesh through a coup, murdering Sheikh Mujibur Rahman and most members of his family in 1975. In a few years, Bangladesh too started becoming an Islamic regime. After General Ershad became the military dictator of Bangladesh, he formally declared the country as an Islamic Republic in the 1980s.

Around this time, in Afghanistan Islamists started gaining tremendous influence. Riots, atrocities against minorities, especially women, destruction and occupation of their places of worship, draconian laws like the blasphemy law and forced conversions became rampant in many parts of Afghanistan—

like in Pakistan and Bangladesh. Dr Ramesh Kumar, a minority member in the Pakistan National Assembly, had said on the floor of the House in 2015 that on an average 5,000 Hindus had been migrating from Pakistan to India annually due to persecution or fear of it. Many come on valid pilgrimage visas and refuse to return after the mandatory visa period of thirty-five days expires. Of the more than 400 temples in Pakistan, only twenty-odd are functional today. The rise of fundamentalist forces like Jamaat-e-Islami in Bangladesh, patronised by certain political parties, had led to frequent riots and atrocities against minority Hindus and Buddhist Chakmas in Bangladesh through the 1980s and 1990s. These minorities were targeted for attacks in the aftermath of the demolition of the Babri Masjid.

All these developments have contributed to continued migration of minorities from these three countries into India. The World Refugee Report published in July 1993 by the US Department of State had stated that by the end of 1992, India had hosted at least two million migrants and another 4,00,000 lakh refugees. In the two decade or so, the situation in Bangladesh improved due to various reasons including the stand taken by the government led by Sheikh Hasina. In Pakistan, too, there were some nominal efforts due to international pressure like banning of forced conversions by the Sindh provincial assembly and Pakistan government's announcement of restoration of old temples. However, these measures remain perfunctory since rabid Islamist elements still retain influence.

Meanwhile, India is saddled with the challenge of millions of minorities from these countries who have been living on its soil for several decades. Had India been a signatory to UN Refugees Convention 1950, these refugees would have automatically claimed and secured citizenship. But that is not the case with India. Every senior leader had recognised this as an issue. Mahatma Gandhi had said in one of his prayer meetings on 16 July 1947:

> There is the problem of those who, out of fear, imaginary or real, will have to leave their own homes in Pakistan. If hindrances are created in their daily work or movement or if they are treated as foreigner in their own land, then they will not be able to stay there. In that case, the duty of the adjoining province on this side of the border will be to accept them with both arms and extend to them all legitimate opportunities. They should be made to feel that they have not come to an alien land.

Jawaharlal Nehru had gone a step further and said on the floor of the Indian Parliament on 5 November 1950: 'There is no doubt, of course, that those displaced persons who have come to settle in India are bound to have the citizenship. If the law is inadequate in this respect, the law should be changed.' It was Nehru who had given first-ever exemption to persecuted minorities from the neighbourhood the Immigrants (Expulsion from Assam) Act 1950. Indira Gandhi had conceded that the minorities who flooded into India around the time of the Bangladesh war would be absorbed by India. Sadly, none of them completed the process of offering citizenship to those refugees.

CAA 2019 simply fulfils that unfinished agenda of the past governments. To portray it as an act against any community is a gross distortion. Citizenship in India is available to various sections of people under various conditions. Besides citizenship by birth and descent that most Indians enjoy, citizenship can be acquired through registration or naturalisation. Sonia Gandhi had become a citizen through registration. Adnan Sami, a Pakistan national, acquired citizenship on the grounds of his domicile and employment. Nobody is discriminated against in the Citizenship Act of India on the basis of religion. The CAA is an additional category of citizenship to the existing ones.

Another point to be kept in mind is that the CAA is a law applicable retrospectively only, not prospectively. It allows for all those minorities of the said three countries who had fled to India before 31 December 2014 to register for citizenship. Where the other citizenship provisions mandate a domicile of twelve years for the applicants, these minorities will be eligible to apply after living in India for at least six years. Those who come after the cut-off date will be deemed to be infiltrators irrespective of their religion. Calling the law communal and discriminatory is also a gross distortion of the facts. Over 1,50,000 Sri Lankan Tamil refugees live in Tamil Nadu. Majority of them are Hindus and Christians. The CAA doesn't provide any help to them. They have been getting citizenship under the existing provisions. It doesn't apply to Tibetans either.

Several countries in the world enact such laws to address problems arising out of certain historical reasons. Recently, the Austrian parliament has passed an amendment to the Austrian Nationality Act offering citizenship to the descendants of all those Jews who had fled the country during Hitler's Third Reich and Holocaust. It has opened the way for the children, grandchildren and great grandchildren of hundreds of thousands of persecuted Jews to apply for Austrian nationality. Previously, only Holocaust survivors themselves were eligible for citizenship. The new law applies to their descendants too.

Indian Muslims have nothing to be anxious about. This law is in no way applicable to any Indian citizen. India has always hosted all the persecuted people from all over the world. It is in India's DNA. People like Taslima Nasrin are living examples of it. Politically persecuted leaders from the neighbourhood too have always found asylum in India. U Thant of Myanmar and Sheikh Hasina of Bangladesh have all been treated as guests in India. The Opposition is trying to trash this national character of India by provoking communal violence in the country. As in the past, they are trying to use Indian Muslims as cannon fodder in their political games.

The CAA is a standalone act that will address the unfinished issue of the persecuted minorities of the three neighbouring countries. The National Register of Citizens, whenever it is announced, will be a separate law. As the Prime Minister himself emphatically stated, there is no discussion about it in the government at this juncture. Mixing up the two issues is unwarranted and tantamount to intellectual dishonesty.

The CAA is historic in the sense that it will alleviate the sufferings of millions of people who were the victims of the fallout of a sin that we had committed in 1947 by partitioning the country on communal lines. Every sensible person should welcome this act.

36

At the Root of Today's Crisis, an Intellectual Void

'Weak minds discuss people; average minds discuss events; strong minds discuss ideas,' said Greek philosopher Socrates. People and events dominate public discourse because they matter to the bread and butter issues of the people. But then, as Jesus Christ said, man does not live by bread alone. He needs ideas—'God's word,' according to Jesus. We need strong minds to germinate transformative ideas. There will be times when humanity yearns for such ideas. The coronavirus pandemic is one such occasion when the world is desperately looking for fresh ideas to shape its future.

Historically, Europe has been the intellectual kernel of mankind. Several avant-garde ideas originated in the minds of European philosophers and thinkers. In the last few centuries, all the important political ideas that impacted the world extensively came from Europe. From John Locke's Enlightenment to Karl Marx's Marxism, from the Utilitarianism of Jeremy Bentham and John Stuart Mill to the Social Contract tradition of Thomas Hobbs, from Edmund Burke's Conservatism to Frederick Nietzsche's Nihilism—Europe produced many grand political ideas in the last two centuries. The democratic institutions that evolved during the same period are also the product of the continuous churning in Europe's intellectual milieu.

One grand idea that India contributed to world political thought in the last century was Mahatma Gandhi's non-violence. From Martin Luther King Jr to Nelson Mandela to Barack Obama—the list of leaders who admired and adopted non-violence as a political ideology is long. Interestingly, after India's successful experimentation with non-violence in 1947, dozens of countries adopted it and subsequently secured independence. Most of those countries became democracies and the world witnessed a 'democracy boom' by the end of the last century. The collapse of the erstwhile Soviet Union and the end of the Cold War also helped further democratisation.

But the dawn of the 21st century saw matters drifting fast. Democratic deficit and fatigue are setting in with alarming speed. Authoritarian regimes have bounced back with a vengeance. Terrorism, that acquired new dimensions and legitimacy towards the end of the last century, has led to the resurgence of the politics of violence. The first quarter of the 21st century witnessed the rise of 'wolf warriors' and 'lone wolves'.

It is in this political climate that the COVID-19 has struck the world. It has affected all existing political systems, authoritarians and democrats alike, diminishing the credibility of each one. A leaderless and rudderless world is emerging out of these two-decades of churning culminating in the pandemic. What the post-pandemic world needs is not just a new leadership, but also ideas for a new world order.

Regarded for long as the crown jewel of democratic liberalism, the United States (US) is yielding ground quickly and significantly, signalling the decisive decline of those values in the world. In the last three decades, at least two dozen countries have turned authoritarian.

Authoritarian regimes, such as China, have emerged powerful during the same period. Authoritarianism does not affect the people of the respective countries alone. It puts a lot of pressure on others too. Democracies, by very nature, become vulnerable to the onslaught of authoritarianism. In the process, they too gradually turn to authoritarian measures to ward off the challenge of authoritarian regimes. The net result will be a world less liberal and less democratic.

There is a silver lining in the cloud though. Authoritarian regimes, although seemingly dominant at the moment, cannot sustain themselves for long. China is ageing fast. The one-child norm of the 1980s and 1990s has skewed its demography. In a decade's time, it will turn into an evening economy. So will other authoritarian regimes in West Asia for a variety of reasons. With their financial fortunes plummeting due to falling oil revenues, these authoritarian sponsors of terrorism are wilting precariously.

The next ten years will be crucial for the world. It has to not only build new leadership, but also come up with new ideas and agendas. It is here that India has a golden opportunity. India's handling of the COVID-19 crisis has revealed the brighter side of its leadership and society. The combined efforts of the government led by Prime Minister Narendra Modi, extensive efforts by its ubiquitous bureaucracy, and the exemplary discipline and commitment of its 1.3 billion people have helped India manage the pandemic in a manner that has set an example to others.

India's COVID-19 experience has highlighted its inclusive nationalism and humanist development vision. These can serve as the ideas for building a new agenda in a post-COVID-19 world. The pandemic has made many countries insular. That has led to the rise of more authoritarianism in the world. India stood out with its inclusivist democratic policies that have seen the government's popularity going through the roof. This, together with humanist globalism as against materialist and militarist authoritarianism, can set a new agenda for the emerging global order.

India has a decade to prepare itself to play a leading role in building such a world order. That is what the Prime Minister Modi calls Aatmanirbhar Bharat (self-reliant India) and Agenda 2030.

37

Our Lives Matter

Out of the 230 years of its existence, the US constitution had allowed for some form of racial discrimination or the other for almost 175 years. When it was being framed, slavery became a contentious issue between the delegates from the south and the north. Finally, the Constitutional Convention had to settle for a compromise on the issue. James Madison, a founding father and the fourth president, wrote: 'It seems now to be pretty well understood that the real difference of interests lies not between the large and small but between the northern and southern states. The institution of slavery and its consequences form the line of discrimination.'

It took more than seven decades and a civil war to formally end slavery in the US. When Abraham Lincoln was elected as the president of the US in 1860, the nation was heading for a civil war on the question of the abolition of slavery. The end of the Civil War and the defeat of the Confederate forces of the south in 1863 marked the end of slavery for the African Americans. The 13th Amendment to the US Constitution in 1865 had finally ended it.

Slavery had ended, but segregation and discrimination continued. It needed another leader in Martin Luther King Jr, and another century, to finally end racial discrimination, segregation and disenfranchisement. The Civil Rights Act of 1964, promulgated by the Lyndon Johnson administration, had put an end to institutionalised racism.

Yet, the recent developments clearly demonstrate that racism is still an everyday reality in that country. The Black Lives Matter (BLM) movement is a stark reminder to the American leadership that it still suffers from many social and moral anomalies, systemic and societal racism being one of them.

The American leadership never tires of preaching about religious freedom and liberal democratic values to the world. The forked-tongue liberals too miss no opportunity to run down countries like India. Since the identity politics anyway dominates the American discourse these days, it may well be reminded that in its 230-year history, the US has not had a single Hispanic president while Hispanics constitute around 16 per cent of the national population. After 220 years, Barack Obama became the first president of African American descent in 2009 while the African Americans constitute over 13 per cent of the population. Not a single woman could rise to become the president of that country so far. This 'exclusivism', as against the much touted 'exceptionalism', in its ugly form is being questioned in recent weeks. In just seven decades, India has had presidents and prime ministers from different religions and communities, including a couple of women.

While the Black Lives Matter is an anguished cry of the beleaguered African Americans for dignity and security, the violence and statue-pulling entailing it establishes that much-maligned McCarthyism has some truth that liberalism became a smokescreen for the far left. Liberal political philosopher Joseph Nye fumbled when asked recently about the violence. Describing himself as a 'liberal realist', Nye insisted that one should see 'long term' in such situations.

In the US, statues of the Confederate states' leaders were controversial owing to their support for the institution of slavery. Similarly, the statues of slave traders erected centuries ago in the British cities might be seen as a stigma by today's generation. Slavery in the US was a British colonialist practice. The monuments that were being pulled down belonged to the descendants of those colonialists. Countries like India had faced colonisation from the Central Asian lands much before the Europeans like the British and French came. Those colonisers like the Turks and Mughals, too, had erected their monuments here. After Independence, many statues of the British colonial era were removed to a corner of Coronation Park in Delhi. Roads like the Kingsway and Queensway became Rajpath and Janpath, respectively.

But when Aurangzeb Road in Lutyens' Delhi was renamed as A.P.J. Abdul Kalam Marg, Indian liberals frowned at it. 'Respect history,' they pontificated. 'Dangerous trend,' they scowled. By the way, they exult at the statues being pulled down in the US and UK. Worse, they fervently wish for a BLM-type agitation in India. 'Why no Dalit Lives Matter movement in India?' publicly bemoaned one of their ilk.

Attempts by the left-liberal cabal to equate the Indian caste system with the race discourse in the West are not new. India has consistently resisted such moves at the international fora. Unlike the founding fathers of the American constitution, the members of India's Constituent Assembly did not hesitate to take the challenge of social inequality head on. In fact, the committee for drafting of the Indian Constitution was headed by

Dr Bhimrao Ambedkar, who himself had very firm views against practices like untouchability and caste discrimination. Speaking in the Constituent Assembly on the last day, 25 November 1949, Ambedkar had summed up the commitment of the nation to absolute social harmony and rejection of any form of discrimination and injustice in the following words:

> Social democracy means a way of life which recognises liberty, equality and fraternity as principles of life. They are not separate items in a trinity, but they form union of trinity. Without equality, liberty would produce the supremacy of the few over the many. Equality without liberty would kill individual initiative. Without fraternity, liberty and equality could not become a natural course of things. Articles 15 (4) and 16 (4), therefore, intend to remove social and economic inequality to make equal opportunities available in reality. Social and economic justice is a right enshrined for the protection of society.

Countless efforts to instigate social conflicts in the name of caste by the anarchist cabal have failed because of the resolve of the Indian society to uphold inclusiveness together with the social justice activism of the Indian Constitution. Rather than looking for a BLM-type agitation in India, the liberals should be looking for peaceful solution to the BLM campaigners' anguish and agitation.

A majority of the African Americans do not support violence and anarchy. Non-violent methods adopted by Martin Luther King Jr's campaign that had resulted in the two landmark laws in favour of their community, the Civil Rights Act of 1964 and the Voting Rights Act of 1965, still inspire them. 'America has a silent Black majority,' wrote Jason L. Riley, a senior member of the *Wall Street Journal* editorial board and a respected African American journalist; and 'Mr Trump may be unpopular, but so are looting, toppling statues, defunding the police, and allowing armed radicals to take over sections of major cities,' he added, echoing the sentiment of that silent majority.

38

Soft Power Struggles

Joseph Nye, the American liberal political scientist, proposed his soft power theory in the 1980s believing that culture would be a non-coercive power to influence nations. Coming ten years after him, Samuel Huntington, a conservative political philosopher, had a different take. 'To understand current and future conflict, cultural rifts must be understood, and culture—rather than the State—must be accepted as the reason for war. Thus, Western nations will lose predominance if they fail to recognise the irreconcilable nature of cultural tensions', warned the *The Clash of Civilisations and the Remaking of World Order* author.

The statue-pulling spree in the US following the gruesome killing of George Floyd, which spread to countries like the UK, is symptomatic of those tensions. Not just the statues of the Confederate leaders like Jefferson Davis and Robert Lee, but even those of the US President during the First World War and the founder of the League of Nations, Woodrow Wilson and the 15th century sea-farer and explorer, Christopher Columbus came under attack in the US, while the two-time Prime Minister of England and the hero of the Second World War, Winston Churchill became a hated figure for many in the UK, along with the slave trader Edward Colston.

Renowned academic institutions also jumped into these conflicts about history and culture. The University of Texas has removed the statue of Woodrow Wilson along with that of Jefferson Davis, while Princeton University has announced the removal of Wilson's name from its prestigious Woodrow Wilson School for Public Policy.

These actions have aroused much controversy. Pulling down of the statues of Christopher Columbus has offended Italian-Americans who faced oppression in the 19th century. Similarly, the defacement of the statue of Winston Churchill in London has anguished many of his admirers who insist that Churchill was 'a child of the Edwardian age and spoke the language of it', while those opposed to him cite his demeaning words and attitude towards Native Americans, African Americans, Arabs and Indians during his heyday.

Soft power symbols are increasingly becoming sources of conflict negating Nye's perspective and upholding Huntington's view. The Yasukuni Shrine in Tokyo, built by Emperor Meiji in 1869 dedicated to soldiers who died at war, became a symbol of conflict between Japan and China a few years ago. The Confucius Institutes that China has established and its penetration of Western academe are increasingly becoming subjects of heated debate in the West. Nepal too is in search of its own Ram, hinting at the political charge and significance of these cultural conflicts.

Recep Tayyip Erdogan, the President of Turkey, has taken the 'clash of civilisations' to a new height by converting the 6th century Byzantine Greek Orthodox cathedral of Hagia Sophia into a functioning mosque. A century after Mustafa Kemal Atatürk, the father of modern Turkey, ended the Ottoman fundamentalism and declared through Article 2 of the Constitution that Turkey would be a 'democratic, secular and social state', Erdogan wants a return to the Ottoman times.

The Ottoman Empire was a communal and theocratic polity under which minorities like the Jews and Christians were forced into dhimmitude and subjected to a humiliating protection tax called the *Jizya*. That was extended to Zoroastrians in Iran and to Hindus in India too. When the Ottoman regime came to an end after the First World War, Mustafa Kemal launched fundamental reforms in Turkey on the basis of six principles—Republicanism, Pluralism, Secularism, Reformism, Nationalism and Statism. He introduced the Gregorian calendar and restored the primacy of the Turkish language over Arabic. While the creation of the Turkish republic entailed the exchange of populations between Greece and Turkey—1.5 million Greeks left Turkish territories and 0.5 million Turks vacated Greek territories—Kamal Pasha ensured that the migration wouldn't affect the secular character of the modern Turkey that he was building.

Hagia Sophia, then converted to a mosque, was one such symbol that Mustafa Kemal wanted to preserve as part of Turkey's civilisational legacy and secular character. He ended the Islamist claims over it in 1934. Later, the UN had declared it a world heritage site.

Hagia Sophia was the largest church built by the Romans in Constantinople in the middle of the 6th century AD. Throughout the Byzantine period, it served as the basilica of the imperial capital. Things changed when the iconoclastic Ottoman sultans conquered the city in the early 15th century. It was later renamed Istanbul. Like Babur and the subsequent Mughal rulers in India, the first thing that the Ottoman Sultan Mehmed II had done after conquering Istanbul was to enter Hagia Sophia and offer namaz there. Thus began the conflict for control over this millennium-old Christian shrine. The Ottoman period saw the destruction of parts of the cathedral, and in recent decades, there have been repeated claims for control by the Islamists.

Turkey is witnessing the rise of neo-Ottomans under Erdogan today. Friday prayers were offered in the cathedral, the first of which, on 24 July, was led by Erdogan himself. Greeks are naturally angry over Erdogan's decision, so are many Christians. Some commentators in Athens are talking about an impending war between Turkey and Greece, catalysed by Hagia Sophia's new Islamisation but also as a result of the geopolitical tensions in the Mediterranean.

'I think of Hagia Sophia, and I am very saddened,' Pope Francis bemoaned. Expressing its 'dismay', the World Council of Churches in Geneva called on Erdogan to 'reverse his decision'. Erdogan has dismissed all criticism insisting that it was his country's 'sovereign right' and Turkey has the 'will to use' it.

Secular Liberals are stuck. They wanted to zealously preserve the Babri structure and keep the name of Aurangzeb Road. But their peers are on a demolition spree in the US and Britain. They can't very well protest Hagia Sophia's reconversion to a mosque or demand for the restoration of its original Christian character, because then they can no longer logically oppose the restoration of Ram Janmabhoomi at Ayodhya.

Cultures are the soul of nations. But conflicts between cultures are not. No soft power, nor hard power, but 'smart power' is what we need to prevent those conflicts.

39

Challenges to Global Governance

The challenge to global governance comes today from the decay of the very institutions created for that purpose some seventy-five years ago. This is the 75th year of the creation of the United Nations Organisation or UNO. The UN was the brainchild of the US President Franklin D. Roosevelt, who first shared the idea with Winston Churchill, although FDR was not there to see it come alive.

When the charter of the founding of the UN was being signed on 26 June 1945, Harry Truman, who had just become the President of the United States of America, proclaimed, 'Oh what a great day this can be in history!' Like his predecessor of twenty-five years, President Woodrow Wilson, Truman also believed that the countries in the world would overcome differences and come together 'in one unshakable unity of determination—to find a way to end wars.'

Speaking at the UNGA in 1950, Truman said: 'The United Nations represents the idea of a universal morality, superior to the interests of individual nations. Its foundation does not rest upon power or privilege; it rests upon faith. They rest upon the faith of men in human values—upon the belief that men in every land hold the same high ideals and strive toward the same goals for peace and justice.'

Today, those words sound like a dream statement from the other world. The UN became almost everything that Truman did not want it to become. In the process, it has lost its sheen and relevance.

Global governance needs to be thought of afresh. The ideas and institutions have to be new to represent the 21st century reality. The institutions of global governance that were created in the middle of the last century do not represent the emergent new global power order anymore. The global power axis has shifted away from the Pacific-Atlantic region to the Indo-Pacific region in this century. Yet the UN is still dominated by the Western powers. Four out of the five permanent members are from the West, whereas the East is the global powerhouse today. The only country to represent the Eastern world is China.

Freedom from wars and striving for peace were the driving force behind the creation of the UN in the last century. Towards that end, it was visualised that a few powerful countries, the permanent members, should have more than equal standing in the world order with a power of the veto.

But the world has transformed since then. We moved from the lofty ideals of the UN to Cold War bipolarity to ambitions of unipolarity to a facade of multipolarity to finally a heteropolar world today. States and non-state actors like multinational corporations, religious groups, social NGOs and even the terrorist groups have emerged as new poles.

This new world order calls for new institutions and also a new agenda. From a country aspiring to become the lone pole in the world, the US has decided to withdraw into its own shell. '21st century world doesn't belong to globalists; it belongs to patriots,' declared President Trump at the UN last year. China under

President Xi Jinping, on the other hand, aspires for the 'Middle Kingdom' status; yet the COVID crisis has certainly affected its standing in the world.

The new institutions that emerge in the post-COVID world should offer greater say for countries in the Indo-Pacific region like India. The 20th century global agenda items like security alliances, multilateral trade and commerce arrangements etc., although important, should take a backseat and new agenda items like climate change and environment, universal healthcare, new and frontier technologies and rules-based world order should come to the forefront on the high table of global governance.

In the 21st century, with the shift in the global power axis, the Indian Ocean has emerged as an important region. It is the lifeline for India. Centrality of the Indian Ocean to regional geopolitics cannot be ignored; and centrality of India to the Indian Ocean too cannot be overlooked. Similarly, the centrality of the Indo-Pacific to global geopolitics cannot be understated; and centrality of the ASEAN powers to the Indo-Pacific too needs to be acknowledged.

In the emerging new global order, India has ambitions to rise as an influential and responsible power. India is home to the world's most ancient knowledge system called the Vedas. From time immemorial, India has championed the cause of environment, healthy living and a rules-based social order called Dharma.

The COVID pandemic has underscored the need for an urgent re-look at the issues related to environment protection and holistic living. Prime Minister Narendra Modi champions the cause of the environment and climate change. India leads the world in non-renewable energy and other climate change issues. He has also championed the spread of yoga—the Indic knowledge system of holistic living. India's traditional wisdom, coupled with the rise of India's collective national consciousness under Prime Minister Modi, will help in catapulting the country into playing a significant role in the making of the post-COVID new world order.

India is the world's largest democracy with impeccable democratic credentials. Prime Minister Modi has handled the COVID crisis very efficiently by exploiting the democratic potential of the country, thus setting an example to the rest of the world.

In the post-COVID new world order, India's mantra of 'Human Centric Development Cooperation', as enunciated by Prime Minister Modi, should become the sacro missionem for the world.

40

When Democracy was Unshackled

American novelist David Foster Wallace began his commencement speech at the Kenyon College of liberal arts in Gambier, Ohio with an instructive story. Two young fishes were swimming along and bumped into an older fish swimming the other way. 'Morning, boys! How's the water?', asks the older fish. The two young fishes continue to swim on, and eventually, one of them asks, 'What the hell is water?'

Reality, for many, becomes so obvious sometimes that they fail to appreciate its value. People in many democracies behave like those young fishes today. They don't realise that with all its defects, democracy is the best available form of government.

Democracy, a Herodotus-era institution of the 'rule of the people', took wing only in the last seven decades. There were 137 autocracies and just twelve democracies in 1945. Bolstered by the victory of the democratic Allied forces, more and more countries turned democratic. By 2001, this number grew to eighty-eight and equalled autocracies. Today, the world has more than a hundred democratic countries while eighty are autocracies.

But democracies are in decline. In the last two decades, more and more countries have become less and less democratic. The Economist recently reported that only twenty-two countries can be called true democracies, while another fifty-three countries can, at best, be described as flawed democracies. More than half of the countries in the world are either semi-autocracies or downright dictatorships.

Liberal democracies are facing multiple challenges. This pandemic has become an excuse for some leaders to usurp more powers and become more authoritarian. The rise of the far left and left-liberal anarchist forces, wanting to destroy mankind's valuable possession of democracy, is also discernible in many countries. Postmodernist scholars are trying to dub democracies pejoratively as populist. They argue that democracies are posing a 'danger' to 'our freedom'. They seek to pit people against democracy.

It is nobody's case that democracies are perfect. There is no single definition of democracy that is universally acceptable. There are 'illiberal democracies' as Fareed Zakaria pointed out and 'liberal un-democracies' as Yascha Mounk wrote. But the alternative to democracy, historically, has only been authoritarian dictatorships. When societies fail to appreciate the value of democratic principles, either dictators are created or anarchy reigns. It also happened, albeit just for less than two years, in India.

Forty-five years ago, on this day, 25 June 1975, India's democracy was shackled by Prime Minister Indira Gandhi. Citing 'internal disturbance' and 'imminent danger to the security of India' as the reasons, she invoked Article 352 of the Constitution and declared a state of internal emergency. The country was pushed into a dictatorship that lasted for twenty-one months. Fundamental rights were suspended. Over 1.4 lakh people were detained, including opposition party leaders. The media was gagged, and even the higher judiciary became a pliant handmaiden of Indira Gandhi. The entire country was converted into a prison of fear. Indira Gandhi's loyalist attorney general, Niren De, had ominously told the Supreme Court that the Emergency gave powers to the government even to take away the life of a citizen—and yet not be answerable to anybody. Citizens' lives and limbs were under threat.

As months passed by, the Stockholm Syndrome set it. Many eminent journalists and writers were singing paeans to the government. 'When asked to bend, they crawled,' L.K. Advani, who spent the entire duration of the Emergency in jail along with colleagues such as Atal Bihari Vajpayee, commented wryly: Hitlerian fascism was reincarnated in Indira's Emergency.

Hitler, after getting elected to the Reichstag—the Lower House of the Weimar Republic—in 1933, had made his National Socialist Party redundant. Senior party leaders were made inconsequential in Hitler's Third Reich. Sycophants and courtiers replaced them. Joseph Goebbels, the propaganda chief, became the most powerful leader due to his proximity to the Fuhrer. A systematic campaign against Jews was unleashed, culminating in their genocide towards the end of the Reich.

Something similar had happened in India during those years. Vidya Charan Shukla, minister for information and broadcasting, became the new Goebbels. Sanjay Gandhi emerged as the super prime minister with a coterie of officials running the show. A systematic Islamophobic campaign was unleashed by this coterie. Sanjay and his coterie became infamous for their forced sterilisation programmes. Corruption and sycophancy had reached unforeseen heights. Dev Kant Barooah, president of the Congress during those years, had acquired sycophantic notoriety by coining the slogan 'Indira is India and India is Indira', something on the lines of the mandatory 'Heil Hitler' salute.

If India's millennials take to the streets today with anarchist slogans, that is because they are like those young fishes in the water, who have never seen the dark side of a dictatorship. Thanks to the valiant fight against the draconian Emergency by the forces that are in power today, the country has enjoyed liberal democracy for four-and-a-half decades. We did not have autocrats partly because of the Gulliverisation of our politics for many years, where smaller parties would pull the strings of power. When a stable majority returned after three decades, the country was in the hands of those who were victims of the Emergency regime's excesses and fought for democracy.

The 'freedom' that the anarchists and their left-liberal cohorts enjoy in the country's media and public life today is because we have leaders in the government who fought for that very freedom and are committed to liberal democratic values, not just as a matter of compulsion but as an article of faith.

INDIA AND THE WORLD

'The Indians nowhere engaged in military conquest and annexation in the name of a state or mother country. The countries conquered militarily by China had to adopt or copy her institutions, her customs, her religions, her language and her writing. By contrast, those which India conquered peacefully preserved the essentials of their individual cultures and developed them, each according to its own genius.'

—George Cœdès

41

Shalom Al Yisrael

Ten months after India secured its Independence, on 14 May 1948, another nation took birth at the other end of Asia. David Ben-Gurion, the great leader of the Jewish people, declared on that day standing in Jerusalem that Israel, a Jewish nation by its Constitution, came into existence on the sacred lands of Yahweh and Moses, called Palestine.

The two nations—India and Israel—have many historical similarities leading up to their respective freedoms from alien rule. Both the lands were under British rule before independence. Both were subjugated for centuries by foreign rulers. In India's case, these were the invaders from Central Asia, the Ghurids, the Ghaznis, the Mughals, and finally, European powers such as the British, French and Portuguese, who had occupied and ruled over large parts of Indian soil. At the other end, the Jews were expelled from their ancestral lands in the first century CE by the Roman empire. They either lived the life of slavery or dispersed all over the world seeking refuge in various countries.

Both had waged decisive battles in the early 20th century culminating in freedom around the same time. Courtesy the British deception, both had to endure a religion-based partition of their respective lands. Both nations had their own leaders who led the popular struggle from the front. In India, it was Mahatma Gandhi, while in Israel, it was David Ben-Gurion. Both were considered moderates in their battles against the British and acquired the title of 'Father of the Nation'. Both countries had a strong streak of armed nationalist wars against their oppressors. In India, there were revolutionaries and the INA, and in Israel, there were groups like Irgun, Haganah and others.

The fervour with which both Indians and Jews had struggled for the freedom of their respective motherland and promised land is also instructive. Every foreign invader was fought ferociously by the contemporary Indian rulers. It took more than three centuries for the Mughals to finally establish their Delhi Sultanate, but it lived for hardly a century-and-a-half. It took more than a century for the British to gain complete control over major parts of India only to return to London in ninety years' time. History tells us that not a single year had passed without the occupiers facing resistance from the natives.

The case with the Jews was slightly different. They were dispersed all over the world in the first century CE, suffered great ignominy in many countries except perhaps in India, and generations had passed without them ever being able to return to their motherland. Yet the successive generations of Jewish leadership had kept the fire of freedom alive in the hearts of millions of Jews across the globe. Every year, the Jews would meet at one place in their respective countries, remember their history, triumphs and travails, and while departing, would shake hands with each other with the slogan: 'Next time in Jerusalem'. For generations on, year after year, the Jews had prayed for their return, never forgot, never gave up. And finally, when that moment came nearer, toward the end of the Second

World War, millions of Jews had started migrating to Palestine leaving behind everything that they had amassed over centuries in their host countries.

Arabs and non-Arab critics argue that the Jewish concept of the 'promised land' was just a piece of mythology and was exploited by the European powers, who hated the Jews for religious and other reasons, to push them to the West Asian corner of Palestine. Fact remains that one of the biggest human migrations happened during the time of Hitler and Second World War from Europe to Palestine. Israelis believe that nearly six million Jews had been exterminated in the most brutal genocide unleashed by Hitler's army during the war. It is known as the Holocaust and in Jerusalem, one can visit the Holocaust Museum to understand the horrors that the Jews were subjected to.

The survivors of the Holocaust and Jews from various other parts of the world started pouring in to the promised land around the time of the war in large numbers. And the final push for securing Israel's independence began then.

Israel's freedom struggle took a different turn from that of India's around this time. Towards the end of the Second World War, the Indian leadership was faced with a challenge. The British had agreed to leave India, but before leaving, they wanted to divide India on religious lines. At that critical juncture, especially when the mobs led by Muslim League were out on the streets of Kolkata and elsewhere creating murder and mayhem, the Indian leadership had developed cold feet. Partitioning of India into Hindustan and Pakistan was agreed to; and finally, it led to the emergence of two independent nations. Years later, Nehru would concede that the leadership was not willing to carry on with the struggle any longer because 'we became old', and hence, agreed for Partition.

What happened in Israel was just the opposite. The Arabs in Palestine were determined not to allow a Jewish state to come into being. Armed struggles broke out all over Palestine with the Jews and Arabs engaging in pitched battles. After the United Nations General Assembly voted in favour of partitioning Palestine and carving out a sovereign state of Israel on 29 November 1947, all hell broke loose. The *fidayeen* groups supported by the Arab League countries led by Egypt had launched armed attacks on Jewish villages and civilians with an avowed objective of annihilating or extraditing the last Jew from the territory of Palestine. 'This will be a war of great destruction and slaughter that will be remembered like the massacres carried out by the Mongols and the Crusaders,' bragged Abdul Rahman Azzam Pasha, the Secretary General of the Arab League.

It was an unequal war for the Jews as they didn't have an evolved state as yet, and they were pitted against several powerful Arab states. It was sheer grit, heroism, patriotism and determination of the Jewish leadership and the people alike that finally led to a newly born state of Israel defeating enemies who were at least five times more powerful than itself.

Israel didn't have a regular army as yet, hence all the youngsters, boys and girls were commissioned into the army. 'A piece of bread, a cup of tea, thrice a day' was the meagre ration that Israel could offer to its fighting youngsters. But they fought without complaining, with empty stomachs. In fact, the ration was the same for even the civilians in Israel in those days. Many elderly Jews used to forgo their ration and remain hungry so that the fighting youngsters could get an extra slice of bed, or an extra cup of tea.

While the Indian leadership had agreed for an atrociously haphazard Radcliffe Line dividing India into two, dividing families, homes and villages in a most irrational manner, the Jewish people under Ben-Gurion's leadership had fought for every inch of territory given to them by the United Nations. There were instances when the Jews sacrificed an entire platoon protecting a lone synagogue in a remote village. Ben-Gurion would insist that Jewish soil cannot once again be allowed to be conquered until the last Jew was alive. 'Israel will not discuss a peace involving the concession of any piece of territory. The neighbouring states do not deserve an inch of Israel's land,' Ben-Gurion would thunder.

In the end, while India's independence came through a bloody Partition under the 3rd June Plan, Israel secured its independence through the blood and sacrifices of millions of its people, but without agreeing to part even an inch of its soil. There was hardly a family at the time of independence in Israel that had not lost a member either in the horrible Holocaust or in the battles against the Arabs during the days of independence. Hence, the Israelis knew the value of their freedom more than any other country in the world.

A tiny country with just over 8.7 million population, out of which about 6.7 million are Jews and 1.8 million Arabs, and surrounded by hostile armies five times its size, what Israel achieved in the last seven decades is an immensely inspirational saga. Israel is today a technological and military superpower. It is one of the world's top twenty highly developed economies with a GDP per capita of over $44,000. With just 0.2 per cent population in the world, the Jews are the largest number of winners of the Nobel Prize, constituting over 20 per cent of the total 900-odd prize winners.

Israel's ways are a subject of animated discussion in the world. The Israelis have all along been at the receiving end of human rights and left-liberal lobbies. The UN has been pitted against them; the Palestine Liberation Authority has more supporters among world powers than Israel does.

Yet, the country moves on with its head held high. For an average Israeli, life is not easy; it is a daily struggle. Militant outfits like Hamas and Hezbollah continuously launch terror attacks inside Israel, targeting civilians as well.

No country is perfect. Israel too has had its share of excesses and mistakes. It has practically nullified the UNGA arrangement by taking over the Palestinian territories of Gaza Strip and West Bank, thus rendering Palestinians stateless. There is still no clarity on whether Israel would agree for a two-state solution to end the vexed West Asian conflict. Its treatment of Palestinians in those territories it occupied after the Six-Day War in 1967 is seen by many as less than satisfactory. In the initial years and decades, it had indulged in random targeted killings of Arabs, and especially the Palestinians, all over Europe and the Middle East on the suspicion of terrorism. Even now, it continues to attract criticism for aggressive and at times excessive use of force against Arab and Palestine targets.

But several of these acts were the result of exigencies under which the Jewish people live. Their precarious living conditions have led them to develop methods that countries in peaceful environment would find objectionable. One needs to be a Jew living in Jerusalem or Haifa or Eilat to understand the rationale behind some of Israel's actions. It is easy to condemn them but difficult to appreciate the dangers of being an Israeli Jew.

What keeps them going? An immense commitment to their land and freedom. An ethereal element of devotion to the promised land is inbuilt in their psyche. A deep-rooted conviction that Israel's future is in the hands of each and every Jew, not just in the hands of a few leaders, motivates them. In that sense, every ordinary Jew is an intense patriot. They have their ideological and political differences. In fact, the Israeli parliament, the Knesset, is the most fragmented parliament in the democratic world. But that doesn't deter an ordinary Jew from working for his nation.

Military training is a compulsory part of every Israeli Jew's life. Once you are eighteen, serving in the Israeli military is mandatory. In fact, those who escape this mandatory training due to health reasons are looked down upon. After serving for a couple of years, most of the Israelis go back to civil life. But they are at the disposal of the Israeli defence establishment at all the times.

'Life is tough. Do you feel bad?' I asked my driver, a thirty-five-year-old Jew, several years ago when I was travelling from Tel Aviv to Jerusalem in the Indian embassy car. 'Yes, sometimes. I completed my military duties. But then I get a call to rejoin military every now and then. I am a married man with children now. I feel bad for my family when I go back to the barracks. Sometimes, I feel that God has been cruel to me. He could have dropped me some 500 miles away in Paris or London. I wouldn't be facing all these problems,' he blurted out. 'Must be very difficult for your family,' I tried to console him. He became stiff. 'But when I join my colleagues in the army, I realise that God has given this duty to me in this life to protect my promised land,' he said to me proudly. It is this spirit that runs Israel. That is why Ben-Gurion used to say that Israel is not a country, but a people.

42

Look beyond Transactionalism

US President Donald Trump expressed anger at India for its high-trade tariffs. His administration complained to the WTO about it. Not that Trump is angry with India alone. He is angry with China as well. And the trade clash between the two countries has acquired serious proportions. Several others too have faced Trump's anger at bilateral or multilateral trade regimes that he sees as unfavourable to the US.

I had written, after Trump's election, that India now has to learn to deal with a 'transactional' president. It is this transactional nature of Trump's dealings that has brought our two countries face-to-face at WTO.

But is the US-India relationship about trade alone? This question needs to be addressed by both countries seriously. Trade plays an important role in our relationship. India's fast growing capabilities in IT, e-commerce and cyber security and massive infrastructure programmes like HIRA—Highways, I-ways, Railways and Airways—offer huge opportunities to US companies. India enjoys distinct advantages, like its massive English-speaking and young population and large-scale skilling campaigns. India is looking to the US for investments and technology transfers as part of its trade relations.

However, both countries must realise that a certain mutual indispensability binds us together. India is an indispensable partner for the US primarily because of its geo-strategic significance. It sits in between two most important regions of the world today. The violent Middle East ending at Af-Pak on its west and the rising Indian Ocean region on the east make India a geo-strategic lynchpin for the US. Former US defence secretary Ash Carter described India as the 'anchor of global stability'.

The Indian Ocean is the most happening region in the 21st century. The global power axis is shifting towards this region. 50 per cent of container trade and 70 per cent of oil shipments flow through this region. The top two of the world's fastest growing major economies are situated in this region. Massive populations with impressive middle class purchasing power make it the most sought after market in the new century.

On the other hand, Af-Pak and beyond, the Arab region, is the most challenging region for the US and the world. Despite military defeats the ideological spread of Al-Qaida and Islamic State continues to pose a challenge to the civilised world.

While this offers India as a huge opportunity to the US, India too needs US as a strategic partner because of its ambition to grow as an influential and responsible global power. The US is an important stabilising power in the Indo-Pacific region, militarily and through diplomatic influence.

India has the world's third largest army, fourth largest air force and fifth largest navy. All three arms are being modernised. With its frontier technological superiority, the US becomes indispensable for India too.

That is why this relationship is described as 'natural alliance'. It is viewed as a 'strategic handshake', representing a broad convergence of geopolitical interests like India's 'Act East' and the US's 'Asian rebalance'. Many have called it the 'defining relationship of the 21st century'.

The US has focussed on overcoming the Eurasian challenge of Soviet Communism in the 20th century by befriending and promoting countries like China. In the 21st century, when the challenge to global peace and stability, and rule-based world order comes from the Indo-Pacific region, it is India that can be the most reliable partner for the US.

As a fast-growing and influential power in the region, India can take the lead in a stable and prospering Indo-Pacific region and also help the US in achieving its counterterrorism objectives in the Middle East.

The 21st century belongs to the Indian Ocean and Indo-Pacific regions. This new century is witnessing the rise of new power alliances, most of them located in the Indo-Pacific region. Tackling this region needs a different approach. The so-called 'American exceptionalism', however successful it might have been in the past in the Americas and Europe, may not work in this region.

In this context, it is interesting to note President Trump's unequivocal statement in his Afghan policy address last year. 'We will no longer use American military might to construct democracies in faraway lands, or try to rebuild other countries in our image. Those days are over now. We are not asking others to change their ways of life, but to pursue common goals that allow our children to live better and safer lives. This principled realism will guide our decisions moving forward,' he said. 'Principled realism' is the keyword in that statement.

India is zealously committed to protecting its sovereign interests while working towards expanding its influence in the Indian Ocean region. It is developing and partnering in a number of regional multilateral networks on the principle of 'multi-stakeholderism'. The US, having scuttled the Trans-Pacific Partnership initiative, must look at supporting and strengthening the India-led and India-partnered initiatives in the region.

India is not averse to building new partnerships with regional powers that help promote India's sovereign as well as global interests like climate change, maritime rule-based governance and so on. It is time India and the US redefined their relationship in the light of the new realities and power shifts of the 21st century.

43

Maa Ganga by Another Name

Some scholars in India consider Mekong a distorted pronunciation of Maa Ganga, Mother Ganges, thus implying that the two rivers, flowing at a distance from each other and enriching large parts of the region, are actually connected with each other through history.

The historian William McNeill described history as, 'The story of ingestion of weaker societies by stronger ones and of rivalries among the strong.' History is witness to the colonisation by superior military powers of large parts of the world. On many occasions, this colonisation happened in the name of a 'civilising' effort made by the West. Military and economic superiority was used to not only colonise parts of the non-Western world, but also impose Western cultural beliefs and practices in the name of bringing modern values to those lands.

The West's quest for imposing its values on the rest of the world gave birth to new theories, like Joseph Nye's 'Soft Power', as distinct from 'Hard Power'. Using non-military and non-political tools to impose one's cultural practices on other societies is described as 'Soft Power'. Here, culture is also a 'power', like military and economic might, which constitute 'Hard Power'. It is fashionable these days to speak of this power casually, but we need to seriously revisit this concept before using it.

The West's unending efforts to create a 'uniform' universal culture based on Western cultural and social values have led to a debate on the fundamental question of whether modernisation means only Westernisation or there can be non-Western models of cultural and civilisational engagement that could enrich human existence.

The history of India and its neighbourhood is replete with examples of how its cultural influence helped native cultures flower and prosper in the region around the country. Here, it was not 'Soft Power' at play, trying to impose an alien value system on the natives; rather, it was a communion of cultures that had benefits for both sides.

The Ganga-Mekong region had witnessed this interplay of cultures at the advent of the first millennium of the Common Era. Ptolemy was one of the first to record this engagement, besides some Chinese scholars in 2nd and 3rd centuries CE. The first recorded engagement was at Funan in 1st century CE. The record says that an Indian traveller by the name of Kaundinya had arrived in the kingdom of Funan, married its princess and established the first ever Indian empire in the region. Funan is identified as the present-day lower Mekong delta, which encompasses southern Vietnam, central Mekong and the Malay Peninsula.

Successive waves of migrations had happened by then, with people having come from Indian kingdoms like Kalinga in Odisha and the Chola domain in southern Tamil Nadu. What is remarkable is that while these migrations led to the establishment of kingdoms by immigrants of Indian origin in the South East

Asian region, from Cambodia to Bali, they are hardly seen as colonisations. The competing influence of the time's Chinese rulers was less charitably viewed by these host communities than the Indian influence.

Contrary to general perception, the populations in the Mekong region didn't belong to the Chinese race. They belonged to diverse races. In his work, *The Indianised States of Southeast Asia*, the French scholar of Southeast Asian history and archaeology George Coedes argues that some of them were Negritos and Veddas, others were Australoids and the Papuan-Melanesians, and still others were Indonesians. 'This fact leads to a clear conclusion: that the earliest inhabitants of Farther India are related to those who inhabit the islands of the Pacific today, and that the Mongolian element in Farther India is of very recent origin,' Coedes argues.

Historians have called the vast area under Indian influence 'Greater India' or 'Farther India'. This description is not fully apt for the important reason that the Indian migrants—royals, sailors, traders, monks—didn't encounter people who seemed 'uncivilised' in the lands that they travelled to. On the contrary, these were organised societies endowed with a value system that had many similarities with their own. Thus the so-called 'Indianisation of Farther India' is an exaggeration because what actually happened was a communion between Indian and native cultures.

Both the Ganga and Mekong regions have been inhabited since prehistoric times by people living in organised settlements, not just foragers but also pastoral and agricultural communities. New archaeological evidence is being unearthed continually now that indigenous scholars are working on it. Historically, the people of both river cultures have migrated, intermingled and engaged in a variety of exchanges.

An important distinction needs to be underscored here. Although several of these countries are in close proximity to China, the Chinese/Mongol influence over these territories has been insignificant, compared to that of India. The reason lies in the way China and India employed methods to influence the populations there. Chinese civilisation was sought to be spread through military conquest followed by the use of official means. The historian K.A. Nilakantha Sastry, in his address to the 9th session of the Indian History Congress in 1946, highlighted that the Indian penetration seems almost always to have been peaceful; nowhere was it accompanied by destruction. Elaborating on this point, Coedes writes:

> Far from being destroyed by the conquerors, the native peoples of Southeast Asia found in Indian society a framework within which their own society could be integrated and developed. The Indians nowhere engaged in military conquest and annexation in the name of a state or mother country. The countries conquered militarily by China had to adopt or copy her institutions, her customs, her religions, her language and her writing. By contrast, those which India conquered peacefully preserved the essentials of their individual cultures and developed them, each according to its own genius. It is this that explains the differentiation, and in a certain measure the originality, of the Khmer, Cham and Javanese civilisations, in spite of their common Indian origin.

This calls for a lot of research and study. Sadly, Indian scholars have simply forgotten that they had vast regions in their extended neighbourhood that had a living civilisation and culture that was partially if not fully of Indian origin. It was left to the French and other European academics in the last century to explore this dimension of India. It is time that scholars in the region take more interest in this subject. From the goodwill that is generated by this cultural communion shall emerge a strong bond between the regions of the Ganga and Mekong for greater engagement and cooperation in the years to come.

44

The Meaning of De-hyphenation

'We have been waiting for you, Prime Minister!' When I heard Prime Minister Benjamin Netanyahu of Israel say this to our Prime Minister at Ben Gurion airport, an old meeting between the two at a New York hotel flashed across my mind.

It was September 2014. Prime Minister Narendra Modi was making his maiden visit to the United Nations to address the General Assembly (UNGA). Elaborate arrangements were underway for the first ever visit of the prime minister that included a big community reception to be attended by 25,000 Indian Americans.

Several meetings at the sidelines with global leaders were also being planned. One of them was with Prime Minister Netanyahu. The request for a meeting at the UNGA came from the Israeli foreign office. But the difficulty was that, as per the schedule, our Prime Minister was to leave the US on the day of the arrival of the Israeli Prime Minister for the UNGA address. The only slot available for the meeting between the two leaders was a Sunday evening, three days before the UNGA address date of the Israeli Prime Minister.

We assumed that the meeting wouldn't be feasible as Netanyahu could not come three days ahead of his UNGA address. Also, for a meeting in New York on a Sunday, he had to leave Israel on Saturday, which, for a practising Jew, is difficult. But, to our surprise, the Israeli side informed us that Prime Minister Netanyahu would be reaching New York for the meeting on Sunday.

Just as we were settling down with a sense of satisfaction over the keen interest of Netanyahu for a meeting with Modi, panic calls started coming in from Jerusalem, four days before Sunday. The Israeli foreign office was informed by someone in the MEA in Delhi that scheduling a meeting with Netanyahu for the Prime Minister, when President Mahmoud Abbas of Palestine was not going to be available for a similar meeting, would be difficult. It would go against the well-established convention, the Israelis were told.

It was hyphenated diplomacy of the Indian foreign policy establishment in action. The time had come for a political call to be taken about this convention. None other than Modi, with his courage of conviction, could have taken that call.

As expected, the Prime Minister brushed aside the conservative view and decided to go ahead with the meeting. That was the first instance of de-hyphenation of our foreign policy. The 'sky is the limit to India-Israel relations' statement recollected by Netanyahu at the Jerusalem airport was from that meeting.

Not just West Asia, there are several other instances where hyphenation has handicapped our ability to forge ties that help our national interests. De-hyphenation has helped us in formulating a more pragmatic foreign policy. Hyphenation, in most cases, is based on romantic ideological reasons. But foreign policy should be guided by pragmatic national and global interest only.

This is a big shift for an establishment that was trained in hyphenated diplomacy. One significant incident in the initial months of our government illustrates the hesitant transition of the establishment from hyphenation to de-hyphenation. Hamas and the Israeli Army were engaged in a serious battle during that time. Missiles were raining in from both sides. India was to issue a statement in the Security Council on the ongoing West Asia conflict. As was the practice, the statement drafted by our foreign office had routinely condemned Israel for using 'disproportionately large' force against 'minor provocation' by the Hamas. As is the wont, the statement had urged 'both sides' to resolve the conflict 'through dialogue'.

That Hamas had fired hundreds of rockets into Israel and that they couldn't hit the targets only because of the high-end Israeli technology called the Iron Dome hardly mattered to those who drafted the statement. Also, the fact that in a war, there won't be anything called 'proportionate force', too, didn't matter. What mattered was the convention that in matters of West Asia, the blame should always be on Israel. In our zeal to uphold that convention, we had even sought to advise Israel to do something that even we wouldn't be doing ever: Dialogue with the terrorist outfit, Hamas. The then External Affairs Minister Sushma Swaraj had to rise in Parliament to clarify that the government wouldn't take sides in the conflict.

It was not the fault of the ministry staffers. It was the convention that had gone on for decades because of our romanticism in foreign policy. Someone had to bring in realism, which Modi did.

It doesn't mean there is any shift in our West Asia policy. We are wedded to our support for the just cause of the Palestinian people and their government. We have supported Palestine in resolutions sponsored by them or other countries at the UN on many occasions in the past few years. That policy will continue.

To attribute our de-hyphenation to ideology and insinuate that it is anti-Muslim smacks of the communal mindset and lack of knowledge about foreign policy on part of the accusers themselves. In our pragmatic de-hyphenated foreign policy, we are friends with Iran and Saudi Arabia at the same time; US and Russia at the same time. China, Philippines, Japan, Vietnam—all of them may be friends or foes at various levels; but for us, they are all our friends on a standalone basis. As Henry Kissinger said, 'There are no permanent friends or foes in diplomacy; there are only permanent interests.'

45

Turning down China

Belt and Road is China's most ambitious initiative in history. Popularly known as One Belt One Road (OBOR), this infrastructure project of gigantic proportions attempts to bring under its sway more than 60 countries, from the Scandinavian world to the South Pacific Islands, in its land and maritime versions. The ancient Silk Route is said to be the inspiration for this initiative launched in 2013.

For President Xi Jinping, Belt and Road is a project of personal ambition and honour. His government has not left any stone unturned to make it a reality in a span of a few years. In the first three years, various projects have seen the signing of contracts worth more than a trillion US dollars.

In a world of competing economic and trade alliances, OBOR has overtaken many others active in the region and beyond. The European Union has some 27 member countries; the Organisation of Petroleum Exporting Countries (OPEC) has 13 countries; the East Asia Summit has 18 countries; even a religious grouping like the Organisation of Islamic Cooperation (OIC) has only 57 countries as members. APEC, TTP, SCO—none comes anywhere near the Belt and Road initiative which boasts of the involvement of more than 60 countries.

By all means, this is singularly the biggest constellation of nations in the 21st century. One prominent nation missing in this mega show is India. Like other countries, India too was invited to the Beijing conclave, with invitations reaching six different ministries for participation in various forums during the summit. The Chinese were hopeful till the last moment about Indian participation. But the government of India decided not to send its representatives to the summit.

Belt and Road is essentially a Chinese project. Two major Chinese financial institutions are supposedly taking responsibility for arranging the necessary finances for participant nations. When completed, the rail, road and maritime routes of this project are expected to boost bilateral and multilateral trade in a big way.

Where the project is a matter of pride for the Chinese leadership, it is also mired in controversy over sovereignty questions and fears about debt servicing obligations. Projects like this one, involving multiple countries, are launched only after proper deliberations among the beneficiary countries and after addressing their concerns.

In the case of Belt and Road, however, the Chinese have opted for a different course. They first announced the project and then initiated the dialogue process with various stakeholder nations. It suited some; for some, like Nepal, it is too big a proposal to be rejected. India is probably the only country that didn't find it virtuous or beneficial to join this mega alliance.

India's reservations need to be looked at from the sovereignty perspective. China routinely threatens countries when it finds issues even remotely connected to its own sovereignty question being 'violated'. Not just China, no country compromises with its sovereignty for the sake of some trade and commerce interests.

India's Achilles' heel is the China-Pakistan Economic Corridor, popularly known as CPEC. The CPEC is seen as a part of the Belt and Road initiative although it started much earlier. In fact, when the Chinese entered into an agreement with Pakistan in 1963 to build the Karakoram Highway in the Pakistan occupied Kashmir (PoK) region, India had vociferously objected to it on the very question of sovereignty. The region through which the highway was to pass belonged to India and has been under the illegal occupation of Pakistan. The Chinese side, thus, has full knowledge of India's concerns about the region.

The CPEC today passes through the same region of PoK called Gilgit Baltistan (GB). India has time and again raised its concerns over Chinese activity in the region, the latest being in 2011 when information came out about the presence of thousands of Chinese troops in the region. Adding insult to injury for India is the very name of the project, CPEC, although the region through which it passes doesn't belong either to Pakistan or to China. In such a scenario, for India to participate in the summit would have meant acceptance of the CPEC proposition.

There is no reason to assume that India's decision will affect bilateral relations with China adversely. Both India and China have a mature leadership under Modi and Xi. Both work together on many other multilateral forums like the Shanghai Cooperation Organisation (SCO), Asian Infrastructure and Investment Bank (AIIB), BRICS Forum, etc. In bilateral relations, there are certain irritants that have either been inherited over time or are a result of realpolitik. That includes China's position on Pakistan and terrorism sponsored by it on Indian soil. India hopes that China appreciates its concerns and takes mutually satisfactory and reassuring measures.

However, being not just a nation but a civilisation in itself, China has time and again betrayed its own style in diplomacy. In his book *The Hundred-Year Marathon: China's Secret Strategy to Replace America as the Global Superpower*, Michael Pillsbury suggested that Chinese strategists have a definite road map for their country to overtake all other world powers, including the US, by the time their Maoist Revolution completes a hundred years in 2049, becoming the sole super power. But President Jinping seems to be a man in a hurry. He wants to achieve it much earlier.

As pointed out by the *Economist*, China today talks not in terms of the China Model or the Beijing Consensus as it used to. The terminology used these days is 'China solution' and 'guiding globalisation'. Its initiatives, including OBOR, need to be viewed from the perspective of these newly coined phrases.

46

New India, Different China

Chinese reaction to the Dalai Lama's latest visit to Tawang varied in tone and tenor from previous occasions. There are reasons for that. *Global Times*, one of the most influential media organs in China, carried a provocative editorial on India in which it asked the rhetorical question: Is India capable of withstanding a 'geopolitical' onslaught from an economically and militarily stronger China?

'With a GDP several times higher than that of India, military capabilities that can reach the Indian Ocean and having good relations with India's peripheral nations, coupled with the fact that India's turbulent northern state borders China, if China engages in a geopolitical game with India, will Beijing lose to New Delhi?' it asked mockingly.

The provocation was the visit of His Holiness the Dalai Lama to Tawang in Arunachal Pradesh. The Dalai Lama's visit was purely religious and spiritual. He has himself clarified that the visit was a routine one like the ones he had undertaken to that state on six earlier occasions. He restricts himself to preaching and sermons most of the time during such visits and occasionally participates in other events. Even in such secular programmes, the Dalai Lama's discourses are usually on universal wisdom and the greatness of the ancient Indian knowledge systems, etc. He hardly raises political issues, much less the happenings in Tibet or China.

Yet, every time he has visited Arunachal Pradesh, the Chinese media has reacted. Even the visits of other Indian leaders have attracted the umbrage of the Chinese. Whether it was President Pratibha Patil's visit or that of Prime Minister Manmohan Singh subsequently, they attracted criticism of varying degrees from the Chinese side. The Indian side also routinely rubbished the criticism as unwarranted interference in the internal affairs of our country.

But there was a difference in the Chinese reaction at that time. It was more aggressive; almost bordering on an open threat. It not only talked about the superior military and economic strength of China, but also issued a veiled warning about the situation in J&K.

One important reason could be the tussle over who the next Dalai Lama would be. The Chinese have already installed their own Panchen Lama, who is regarded as next only to the Dalai Lama in the Tibetan spiritual hierarchy. His Holiness the 14th Dalai Lama is at an advanced age. As per the Tibetan Buddhist tradition, indications about the next Dalai Lama would be left behind by the present one. The 14th Dalai Lama has so far not given any clear indication about the next one. He has fleetingly made statements like 'the next Dalai Lama could be a woman' or 'the Tibetans have to decide about the future of this institution of Dalai Lama'.

But the Chinese seem to have their own worries about the matter. They seem to especially suspect that the Holiness might choose someone from India, or even from Arunachal

Pradesh, as his successor, thus leaving the movement for Tibetan independence with another leader. There were occasional suggestions that China is contemplating declaring the next Dalai Lama, which have been rubbished by the Holiness himself. He has categorically stated that China can't do another Panchen Lama with the Dalai Lama.

The other reason could be its territorial claims over Arunachal Pradesh. Here, it needs to be mentioned that Chinese territorial claims over Arunachal Pradesh are of recent origin. During the 1962 war, Chinese troops had annexed half of what used to be called NEFA in those days. Their troops had reached up to Tezpur. New Delhi had almost concluded that Assam fell to them. Nehru infamously delivered a radio address to the people of Assam, bidding farewell to them.

But then the Chinese side announced unilateral ceasefire on 21 November 1962. Surprisingly, they decided to stay put in the areas they had annexed in the western sector in Ladakh, but withdrew to the pre-1962 positions in the eastern sector. Thus, instead of annexing Assam, the Chinese troops vacated all of western Arunachal Pradesh, including Tawang. This decision of Mao became controversial in China; many believed that Mao was wrong.

Arunachal Pradesh became disputed in Chinese eyes only after the formal joining of Sikkim in the Indian Union in 1975. The Chinese side started raising the status of Arunachal Pradesh regularly since 1978. They have invented claims as far-fetched and fantastic as the Chinese people having the graves of their forefathers in Arunachal Pradesh and they would wish to have that territory as part of their motherland.

But the Chinese reaction in 2017 is markedly different in tone from previous occasions. I am reminded of the term 'Finlandisation', coined by the German political scientist Richard Lowenthal in 1961. In the aftermath of the Second World War, Finland chose to follow a policy of not standing up to the Soviet Union militarily or economically, even while the country had remained a part of Allied Western Europe. 'Finlandisation' has become a pejorative of sorts that entails a gloomy prospect of a future 'when West European nations may discover themselves militarily surrounded, economically beleaguered and psychologically isolated, having to draw the consequences', as Walter Hahn put it.

The Indian response thus far has been on the lines of Finlandisation, a classic example narrated by a senior Indian columnist: 'In 2009, largely unnoticed by the Indian media, China and India had drifted close to war over the Dalai Lama's proposed visit to open a hospital in Tawang town. Conflict was averted when Prime Minister Manmohan Singh readily acceded to a request by Premier Wen Jiabao at an APEC meeting in Hua Hin, Thailand, to keep the international media out of Tawang and prevent it from giving the visit international significance.' Probably the Chinese feel that India is coming out of this Finlandisation under Prime Minister Narendra Modi, and hence, the serious warning.

47

Wolf Warrior Diplomacy

'*Yi pai hu yan*,' sneered the Chinese foreign minister when US Secretary of State Mike Pompeo said the regime in China was comparable to that of the Soviet Union—'a communist, tyrannical regime', but the Chinese people 'are a great people'. The Chinese phrase is generally derogatory and can be interpreted mildly to mean 'a bunch of nonsense'.

Making a distinction between the people and the regime in China is a favourite pastime for many in the US. Mike Pottinger, the US Deputy National Security Advisor, addressed the Miller Centre of the University of Virginia. Speaking in fluent Mandarin, Pottinger recalled the student protests at the Tiananmen Square a hundred years ago on 4 May 1919 that had led to the Chinese leadership refusing to sign the Treaty of Versailles. 'Weren't they a broadside against the Confucian power structure that enforced conformity over free thought? Wasn't the goal to achieve citizen-centric government in China, and not replace one regime-centric model with another one? The world will wait for the Chinese people to furnish the answers,' he told the students, ostensibly suggesting that the spirit of the May Fourth Movement would return in China.

One should not be surprised when Chinese leaders sneer at such suggestions. Those suggestions betray a general lack of understanding about China. Francis Fukuyama, in an article in Foreign Policy, traces the authoritarian history of China in the last two millennia and aptly concludes that the so-called revolution, if any, will come not from the bottom, meaning the people, but from the top—the ruling oligarchy.

China is a great civilisation. Yet, under the Chinese Communist Party (CPC), it is a nation driven more by history. China could be understood only by understanding Mao Zedong's Long Revolution from 1911 to 1949. British historian Eric Hobsbawm had described 20th century as a 'short century' spanning from the start of First World War in 1914 to the collapse of the Soviet Union in 1991. The Chinese scholars further shorten it by describing it as the 'Short century of the Long Revolution'. And the message of that revolution is the domination of the state.

Revolutions came to China, but from the top. The Cultural Revolution was imposed on hapless Chinese people by Mao and his Gang of Four. Top leaders including Deng Xiaoping were sent away to the countryside, so was a young Xi Jinping. Later revolutions were led by these two Cultural Revolution veterans. However, the two drew opposite inspirations from it.

Deng came to power in 1979 and became a major reformer. His 'four modernisations' led China to become a 'socialist state with market economy'. He laid the foundations for the modern-day economic power of China. It may be worthwhile to recall that when Deng began his reforms, China's GDP was at $191 billion while India's was $186 billion. Four decades later, China is five times bigger. It was a revolution engineered at the top.

But the same Deng showed utmost cruelty towards the student protestors at the Tiananmen Square in 1989. June 4 was the day when the PLA, under Deng's orders, had ruthlessly crushed the student protests for a more open political system. A less known fact is that behind this brutal repression was a brewing leadership struggle within the CPC. Deng had called for political reforms for the effective implementation of his economic reforms. Two central committee leaders, Hu Yaobang and Zhao Ziyang, who were made the general secretaries of the CPC successively, were at the forefront of drafting the political reform programme. But when student protests broke out first in 1987 followed by the famous Tiananmen Square protests in 1989, the two leaders were purged by Deng. Hu died in 1989 and Zhao was put under house arrest after being removed as the general secretary in 1989.

Popular revolutions are not tolerated in CPC-led China. But top-down revolutions do happen. The latest revolution to export Chinese influence far into the world began with the rise of Xi Jinping in 2013. His rise as the supreme leader was followed by the insertion of 'Xi Jinping Thought on Socialism with Chinese Characteristics in a New Era' into the CPC constitution. Its main thrust is twofold: Making China a nation with pioneering global influence and building a world-class military force.

The greatest challenge to Xi's thought came in 2020 in the form of the pandemic. Internal discord seems to have been suppressed. But external pressures, especially from the US, continue. Faced with such situations in the past, China had reacted in a way that Sun Tzu would describe as 'the highest form of warfare is to attack the strategy itself; the next, to attack the alliances'. When the Sino-Soviet relations deteriorated after 1956, leading to Mao calling Nikita Khrushchev a revisionist, China had used war with

India, a perceived Soviet ally, in 1962 to convey to the Soviets its military superiority.

Besieged with multiple problems—Hong Kong, Taiwan and the US externally, and economic and pandemic challenges internally—Xi seems to be returning to Mao's Red Book. In the famous Chinese movie *Wolf Warrior II*, the protagonist, Leng Feng, a retired Chinese army commando, is seen rescuing people from a civil-war torn African country under the heel of an American mercenary. In the final scene, the fictional hero holds the Chinese flag aloft, while the awestruck enemy backs off seeing the flag. Wolf Warrior diplomacy is a phrase popular in China these days. Aggression is the panacea for both domestic and international challenges, Xi appears to think.

This historical China is what we confront on the borders and in diplomatic circles. India has matured its border management and diplomatic manoeuvres over the last few years. 'Proactive diplomacy together with strong ground posturing' is its new mantra. From Doklam in 2017 to Galwan Valley and Pangong Tso in 2020, India has been consistent. A mature China that does not resort to 1962 tactics, this time replacing Khrushchev with Trump, nor is bent upon provoking nationalist sentiments back home to ward off leadership challenges, would help roll back the situation.

48

The Heat in Beijing

This coronavirus pandemic is catalysing major geopolitical upheavals. There appear to be not many takers in the world, at least among the big powers, for the UN Secretary General António Guterres' appeal on 23 March, 'To the warring parties: Pull back from hostilities. Silence the guns; stop the artillery; end the airstrikes. This is crucial to help create corridors for life-saving aid, open windows for diplomacy and bring hope to places among the most vulnerable to COVID-19'.

Guns are not silenced. The artillery is blazing. In less than three decades, the talk of a new cold war has returned. From *Washington Post* in the US to *Daily Sabah* in Turkey to *Strait Times* in Singapore to *The Australian* in Australia—so many are talking about it. Kevin Rudd, former Australian Prime Minister, too had alluded to it in his article in *Foreign Affairs* magazine.

The last Cold War began several years after the end of Second World War. At least in the fight against Hitler and Mussolini, there was greater unity in the world. Hitler could not have been defeated had Roosevelt not jumped in and Stalin not changed sides. But now, we are still in the midst of the coronavirus pandemic. The need of the hour is greater unity. It is ominous to hear the increasing cacophony over the new cold war at this juncture.

Recently, the World Health Assembly (WHA) had witnessed the cold war pre-run at its annual session. Issues like investigating the origins of coronavirus and readmitting Taiwan as an observer have led to deep schisms and open mudslinging among the big powers. The Bahamas-led WHA has not agreed for an independent inquiry to investigate the virus origins, nor has it taken up the Taiwan issue on the agenda. While there is palpable exuberance in Beijing, it is radio silence in Canberra and Washington, D.C. The official mouthpiece of the Chinese Communist Party (CPC), *Global Times* has used choicest epithets against President Trump and the US. 'This is pure international hooliganism,' it accused the US, and mocked President Trump saying he was 'out of control' and using 'witchcraft'.

Incidentally, China was instrumental in making Taiwan an observer at the WHA from 2009 to 2016. There was a pro-China KMT government in power in Taiwan then. After the pro-freedom DPP returned to power in 2016, Taiwan withdrew refusing to be called as Chinese Taipei.

India's Cold War Experience

India's brush with the Cold War in the last century was brief. It happened during the 1971 war with Pakistan. Nixon's antipathy for India had led to the US's tacit support for General Yahya Khan, the Pakistani dictator at that time. Yahya Khan had indulged in a genocide of the Bengalis in East Pakistan, while Nixon looked the other way.

In the end, Pakistan lost the war and territory, and Nixon his moral stature. A telegram sent by Archer K. Blood, the US consul general in Dhaka during those fateful months, had helped in exposing the immoral behaviour of the Nixon-Kissinger duo. Blood had repeatedly warned the US establishment about the goings-on in East Pakistan. His warnings fell on deaf ears. Finally, Blood had taken on the US leadership through a terse telegram sent to the State Department challenging its silence over the genocide.

'Our government has failed to denounce the suppression of democracy. Our government has failed to denounce atrocities. Our government has failed to take forceful measures to protect citizens while at the same time bending over backward to placate the West Pakistan-dominated government and to lessen any deservedly negative international public relations impact against them. Our government has evidenced what many will consider moral bankruptcy ...,' Blood's telegram concluded. Blood was punished for his bluntness and removed from Dhaka.

Tale of Two Telegrams

The Cold War was immoral and unethical. The Western and Eastern blocs had used all methods to outdo one another, bringing horrible misery to the people in many countries. Those in the opposite camps had suffered anyway, but those, like India, that weren't part of any camp, too, were not spared. It had ended over the dead bodies of over twenty million people.

It is instructive to learn about how the Cold War had begun. Historians hold two telegrams responsible for the rise of Cold War politics in the last century. They are called Kennan and Novikov telegrams. Like the Blood Telegram, they too were based on the local assessment of the diplomatic officials of the US and the USSR. Kennan was the deputy chief of the US mission in Moscow while Nikolai Novikov was the Russian ambassador in Washington, D.C. Kennan's assessment of the post-War strategy of Stalin, which was contained in a long telegram of 8,000 words that he sent to Washington in 1946, was largely responsible for the US initiating Cold War measures, including the formation of the anti-Soviet NATO. Just a few months after Kennan's 'Long Telegram', Novikov sent his assessment of Truman administration to Moscow in another telegram that became known as Novikov Telegram. Sent in September 1946, Novikov Telegram warned Stalin that the US was determined to contain the spread of the 'democratisation efforts' of Stalin and planning to establish bases in the capitals of USSR's neighbours. The two telegrams had set the stage for the Cold War in the last century.

Cold War Rhetoric

Similar situations are unfolding in Beijing and Washington now. *Reuters* has reported that an influential Chinese think tank, the China Institute of Contemporary International Relations (CICIR), affiliated with the top Chinese intelligence body, the Ministry of State Security, had presented a confidential report to the Chinese top leadership in which it predicted a massive anti-China wave across the world surpassing the sentiment in the aftermath of 'the 1989 Tiananmen Square crackdown'. It had even predicted an armed confrontation with the US.

Temperatures are on the rise in Beijing over such reports. 'China needs to expand the number of its nuclear warheads to 1,000 in a relatively short time,' wrote Hu Xijin, the influential editor-in-chief of *Global Times*. The Chinese media is also talking about the US's efforts to 'encircle' China. Political commentators in China have started comparing the CICIR report with the Nikolai Telegram hinting at the start of a new cold war.

Meanwhile, on the US side, with elections round the corner, both the Republicans and the Democrats are upping the ante against China in variable decibels. Adding to the rhetoric, a purported report by the Pentagon, submitted last month to the White House, has surfaced in sections of the Western media that talked about a series of simulated war games conducted by it against the Chinese military targets. The war games had led to the Pentagon concluding that the US forces would be 'defeated in a sea war with China and would struggle to stop an invasion of Taiwan', claimed the report.

Roadmap for Peace

The National People's Congress (NPC), the titular Chinese parliament of over 3,000 representatives, commenced its delayed annual ten-day meeting on 22 May. Premier Li Keqiang presented the country report to this largely rubber stamp legislative body. Many suspected that the Chinese leadership would use the forum to further augment nationalist sentiments in the country. The re-elected pro-freedom Democratic Progressive Party leader Tsai Ing-wen, the *bete noire* of President Xi Jinping, inaugurated her second term just two days before the NPC in a subdued way after the setback at WHA. That could have become an added spark for shrillness at the NPC.

There are many in India and globally who would hope that all was not well inside China and there could be another Tiananmen-like uprising. It must be remembered that in its long history, the Chinese society has lived under one kind of authoritarianism or the other. As Francis Fukuyama pointed out, they glorify their authoritarian history by way of escorting visiting country heads to places like terracotta warriors in Xian. This place has the tomb of Shang Yang, the chief minister of the pre-Christian-era Qin dynasty who had introduced a proto-totalitarian governance model based on the premise that all human beings are born bad. China is a 'historic nation'; it values a continuum in its history. The CPC's authoritarianism is no different from Shang Yang's. It can change through the struggles not at the bottom, but at the top, opines Fukuyama. That could be a long wait as President Xi has consolidated his position substantially.

On the other side, Trump's election strategists seem to have decided upon making China the centrepiece of their re-election campaign. As the new cold war clouds gather over the horizon, countries like India have to weigh their options carefully. NAM-type 'neither here, nor there' neutrality is no longer feasible because the new cold war is going to play out in India's immediate neighbourhood. Instead, India could become the fulcrum for countries in the Indo-Pacific region. Prime Minister Narendra Modi has already laid out his vision when he said at the Shangri La Dialogue in 2018: 'India's own engagement in the Indo-Pacific Region—from the shores of Africa to that of the Americas—will be inclusive. It translates into five S's: सम्मान (respect); सम्वाद (dialogue); सहयोग (cooperation), शांति (peace) and समृद्धि (prosperity).' India's hardball agenda should be to engage with countries on 'peace, with respect, through dialogue and absolute commitment to international law,' as Modi put it.

49

Going beyond Panchsheel

The biggest problem in Sino-Indian relations is the utter lack of ingenuity and innovativeness. Six decades after the formal engagement through Panchsheel and five decades after the bloody disengagement due to the war of 1962, the leaders of both the countries still struggle to come up with new and out-of-the-box answers to the problems plaguing their relationship.

When there are no new ideas, one would resort to symbolism and rituals. These rituals and symbolic actions are projected as the great new ideas to kick-start a new relationship. However, there is nothing great nor new about these actions. They are the very same worn out and tried-tested-and-failed actions in the last several decades.

Panchsheel itself is one such ritual that successive Indian governments have unfailingly performed in the last five or more decades. Vice President Hamid Ansari visited Beijing on 28 June 2014 to uphold India's commitment to the ritual. The occasion is completion of six decades of the signing of the Panchsheel Agreement.

It was on 28 June 1954, roughly two months after the formal signing of Panchsheel, that the Chinese Premier Zhou Enlai visited India. He and Prime Minister Nehru had issued a historic statement on that day reaffirming their commitment to the five principles that were enshrined in the Panchsheel that 'would lessen the tensions that exist in the world today and help in creating a climate of peace'.

What exactly was Panchsheel?

Contrary to public perception or propaganda, Panchsheel was actually an agreement between 'Tibetan region of China and India' on 'Trade and intercourse'. It did include five principles like mutual respect, mutual non-aggression, mutual benefit, peaceful coexistence etc, but the very title of the Agreement itself was a big defeat to India.

The British had, at least from the Shimla Agreement of 1912 onwards till they left India, never conceded that Tibet was a part of China. Unfortunately, one of the first foreign policy deviations of the Nehru Government was the signing of Panchsheel wherein India had formally called Tibetan region as 'of China'.

Thus Panchsheel was signed as a treaty of peaceful coexistence over the obituary of Tibetan independence. That was why eminent parliamentarian Acharya Kripalani called the agreement as 'born in sin'.

Rituals Continue

Panchsheel met its watery grave in just three months after its signing when the Chinese were found violating Indian borders in Ladakh area in late 1954. A formal death note was written by Mao a few months before the war of 1962 when he told Zhou Enlai in a mischievous tone that what India and China should practise is not 'peaceful coexistence' but 'armed coexistence'.

The war followed and ended in a huge humiliation and loss of territory to India. It left behind a massive border dispute which continues to haunt both the countries.

However, all this didn't seem to deter the Indian and to some extent the Chinese leadership in continuing with the deception of Panchsheel. History of Sino-Indian relations in the last five decades is replete with instances of violations of sovereignty, mutual animosity, attempts to upstage each other and general ill-will. Mostly, the Chinese were on the wrong side of the so-called Five Principles of Peaceful Coexistence.

Yet the ritual continued through the decades and changing governments in India. Nehru to Narasimha Rao to Vajpayee continued this ritual of paying lip sympathy to Panchsheel during the bilateral visits.

'Only with coexistence can there be any existence,' declared Indira Gandhi in 1983. Her son and the next Prime Minister of India Rajiv Gandhi expressed confidence in 1988 that 'the five principles of peaceful coexistence provide the best way to handle relations between nations'. Narasimha Rao as Prime Minister declared in 1993 that 'these principles remain as valid today as they were when they were drafted'.

While Vajpayee too was forced to continue this ritual, he made a significant difference by refusing to falsely credit China for following Panchsheel. He put extra emphasis on 'mutual sensitivity to the concerns of each other' and 'respect for equality'.

New Framework

While Beijing has celebrated six decades of Panchsheel, it is important to look at a new framework for Sino-Indian relations beyond Panchsheel. Vajpayee laid some foundation for a renewed outlook by emphasising on sensitivity and equality. That can form the basis for the new framework.

The Chinese have a clever way of promoting their superiority and exclusivism. Sinologists describe it as Middle Kingdom syndrome. While Nehru wanted to take credit for Panchsheel, Zhou Enlai told Nixon in 1973 that 'actually the Five Principles were put forward by us, and Nehru agreed. But later on, he didn't implement them'.

The Chinese side also brought in Myanmar—Burma at that time—and entered into a similar agreement with that country also on the same principles in 1954. Thus, they made sure that Panchsheel doesn't have any exclusivity in terms of their relationship with India.

For the Beijing event, the Chinese government invited the President of India as well as the President of Myanmar. General Thein Sein, the Myanmar President was present along with the Vice President of India Hamid Ansari who led the Indian delegation.

Without any malice towards Vice President Ansari, one would notice the downgrading of India's participation in the Beijing event. Beijing was keen on having the President or Prime Minister at the event. But for once, the South Block mandarins seemed to have done good homework in advising the Indian government against sending either of them. The then Foreign Minister Sushma Swaraj too decided to skip the event and chose to visit Dhaka around the same time sending a rather strong signal.

If Prime Minister Modi and President Xi Jinping decide to depart from the Panchsheel framework and embark on a new relationship, both countries would greatly benefit. Both leaders have that ability as both of them come from backgrounds that are markedly different from Nehruvian and Maoist ones. Both enjoy trust and confidence of the people of respective countries. Most importantly, both are seen as out-of-the-box leaders.

India and China can cooperate with each other on the principles of sovereign equality and mutual sensitivity. China has emerged today as an economic superpower, but it is exposed to serious internal and external threats. It is facing problems with almost all of its thirteen neighbours. The fact that China spends more money on internal security than on external security speaks volumes about its internal vulnerability. That way, while India is not that big an economic power as China is, its security apparatus is certainly better placed than China's.

Modi and Jinping can chart a new course in Sino-Indians relations if they are prepared to unshackle themselves from ritualism and symbolism. Both have the ability to do that and the much needed support from the people.

50

China
The Real Foreign Policy Challenge for India

Prime Minister Modi's foreign relations innings began with a bang through the invitation to the heads of the SAARC countries for his swearing-in. The resounding success of that initiative can be gauged from the fact that all but one head of state turned up for the event making it an international relations coup of sorts.

Through this deft move, Prime Minister Modi proved that he understands the external affairs department well enough. He is not all that new to other countries and their leaders. As Chief Minister and even earlier as a party leader, he had visited several countries including China, Japan and the US. His home state became a destination for countless world leaders during his stewardship and he regularly rubbed shoulders with the high and mighty from more than a hundred countries during his Vibrant Gujarat Summit and other events.

His former cabinet colleague and Minister for External Affairs Sushma Swaraj too was no novice to the subject. As the Leader of Opposition in the Lok Sabha, she had had the opportunity to interact with a number of senior world leaders including President Obama. Her visits to Singapore and Sri Lanka as the leader of BJP showed her grip on foreign affairs. Leaders of those countries fondly remember their association with her even to this day. Swaraj's acumen can be appreciated from the fact that Hillary Clinton was greatly impressed by her use of the word 'Act East' as a substitute to India's two-decade-old Look East policy. Borrowing it from Swaraj, Clinton in fact started using it in her subsequent speeches on Asia.

Prime Minister Nawaz Sharif's participation in the swearing-in has raised big hopes in the diplomatic circles in both the countries. India and Pakistan have had chequered relations from day one. Moreover, the BJP is seen as a hardline party when it comes to relations with Pakistan. Given that scenario, it is natural that a lot of discussion took place on whether Modi and Sharif would kickstart a new era in the vexed bilateral ties.

This feverish enthusiasm is understandable. Many Indians have, for several decades, been obsessed with Pakistan. For them the benchmark of success of our international relations is our relationship with Pakistan. They fail to appreciate that India is miles ahead of its failed western neighbour. They also failed to realise that Sharif was not the right man to deliver anything. As Ayaz Amir pointed out in his article in *The News*, while Manmohan Singh took ten years to fail, Sharif may need just two years to collapse. The all-powerful Pakistan Army and the mercenaries of the ISI were already baying for his blood. As President Karzai pointed out the attack on the Indian Consulate in Afghanistan by the ISI cronies on the very day of Modi's swearing-in was more a warning to Sharif than to India.

However, Modi Government should realise that the real foreign policy challenge comes not from Pakistan but from China. India and China have been uneasy neighbours for longer years than India and Pakistan. Unlike Pakistan, China is a big and successful country. Indian leadership should understand one basic truth. It hardly matters in China's context as to how many times our leaders have visited China or vice versa. The notion that diplomacy is all about proximity doesn't hold any water in China's context. Nehru to Nixon had good experience of it.

What plagues our foreign policy with regard to China is the utter lack of knowledge about the Himalayan neighbour in our country. With Pakistan, our obsession is security whereas with China, we are overawed by the talk of development there. Commoners and ministers alike look at China only from the prism of its development and fail to appreciate the complex civilisational traits of that country.

All neighbours are not alike. China is certainly not like any other neighbour. China is not just a country or a government; it is a civilisation. To understand China, our leader should better understand their civilisational behaviour … we should know Sun Tzu's *Art of War*; we should study Confucius. China's policy behaviour is largely shaped by their civilisational experience. Diplomacy, for them, is an art of deception.

In 1954, India and China proclaimed Panchsheel as the basis of our relations as discussed earlier. Successive Indian leaders, including Vajpayee, never missed the opportunity to refer to Panchsheel and 'peaceful coexistence' as enshrined in it in the bilateral talks with the Chinese counterparts. No wonder if the present leadership is also forced to continue the ritual by the MEA mandarins. But we forget that the obituary of Panchsheel was written by Mao in 1962 itself when he told Zhou Enlai that India and China should practise not 'peaceful coexistence' but 'armed coexistence'.

Another important aspect of China to be borne in mind is that, just as in Pakistan, military plays an important role in China too. The Central Military Commission, the all-powerful body that controls the Chinese Military, reports to the CPC more than to the Government of China. While we deal with the government leadership on various bilateral issues, we can't overlook the fact that the view of the military on various cross-border issues is also significant.

Indian government enjoys one advantage in India-China relations, that of the ignorance of the masses in India about the complexities in it. In case of Pakistan, people of India are very aware, forcing government's options to a limited few. Whereas in case of China, no such constraint in the form of popular backlash is going to happen. The very fact that while there were animated debates over whether Nawaz Sharif should have been invited or not continue to this day, there is no such commotion with regard to the phone call or proposed visit of the Premier of China proves this point. But the government must understand that this popular approval borne out of lack of knowledge can become a danger if it decides to take things easy with China.

51

India has a Moral Commitment on Tibet

Till the 1960s, the Chinese were talking about a bilateral settlement on Aksai Chin. The 38,000-square-kilometre area, part of Ladakh region, came under illegal occupation of the Chinese Red Army, which started constructing the Karakoram Highway linking Tibet with Sinkiang region in the 1950s.

Zhou Enlai, the then Premier of China, convinced Jawaharlal Nehru that the McMahon Line is an 'imperial leftover' and hence, China and India should reject it. Under Krishna Menon Plan in 1960, it was even proposed that India should agree for the Chinese control over Aksai Chin while the Chinese on their part would agree for something 'closer' to McMahon Line in Arunachal Pradesh.

This, obviously, was not acceptable to India because China was conspiring to annex Indian territory in exchange for another Indian territory. The proposal failed, war followed; and we formally lost control over the Aksai Chin region.

Subsequently, Sikkim became the theatre of conflict. While India was engaged in a war with Pakistan in 1965, the Chinese PLA was actively making incursions into the Indian territory in Sikkim along the Tibetan border. China blamed India for preventing its sheep from grazing inside the Indian territory, which led to the incursions. There were skirmishes between September and December in 1965 in that region.

Tensions continued along the Sikkim-Tibet border where there was armed conflict in September 1967 near Nathu La Pass when the PLA tried to cross the border in large numbers. Indian troops had successfully repulsed these advances.

By the 1980s, the theatre shifted to the eastern sector and Arunachal Pradesh became the new arena of conflict. While under the so-called Krishna Menon Plan, the Chinese were willing to agree for the Indian claims in the eastern region in exchange for Aksai Chin, in 1980s they started making fresh claims over Arunachal Pradesh.

In 1980, when Deng Xiaoping suggested sector-wise approach to resolving the border conflict between India and China, it was presumed that he was only resuming Zhou's line. However, when the border talks began in 1981, Indian side got clear indications that the Chinese are pursuing a maximalist approach. By 1985, when the 6th round of talks began the Chinese had started making open claims over Tawang in particular and Arunachal Pradesh in general.

What followed gives a clear idea of the Chinese method. There were major border violations by China in 1987 in the Sumdorong Chu Valley where the Chinese had penetrated deep into the Indian territory and constructed a helipad and started bringing in reconnaissance. This had led to a major military build-up and an eyeball-to-eyeball positioning of both the troops.

Tensions ran very high for several years until the Narasimha Rao regime signed a treaty with the Chinese Government in 1993. In a way, this treaty too could be called a victory for the Chinese side, as it had resulted in both Indian and Chinese troops moving out of the Sumdorong Chu Valley and leaving it a neutral region. Once again while the Chinese had to vacate the territory that they occupied, the Indians were forced to vacate what belonged to them.

Almost five decades of efforts to resolve the border issues, it had resulted only in India conceding every time and ending up as the loser. Zhou talked of a 'package deal'; Deng talked of sector-wise approach. We today see neither of them to be relevant anymore. Of the 2500-kilometre border, only peaceful sector is the middle one—namely the Tibet-Uttarakhand/Himachal border—which is not more than about 550 kilometre.

The Chinese refuse to talk anymore about the Aksai Chin. For them, it is a settled fact. What is unfortunate is that even our own leadership stopped talking about it. Rajiv Gandhi visited China in 1988; Narasimha Rao in 1993 and Vajpayee in 2003. The nation has not heard them talk about the occupation despite the fact that there is a unanimous Parliament resolution of 1962 on getting that territory back.

For the Chinese, the obvious policy appears to be to get the maximum territorial advantage of the talks. That is the reason behind their constant harping on Arunachal Pradesh. Even there, the initial claims were only over the Tawang region. These claims were based on the so-called historical aspects like the birth of the 6th Dalai Lama Tsangyang Gyatso there.

But now, the claims extend to the entire state of Arunachal. In 2006, just a couple of weeks ahead of the visit of the Chinese President Hu Jintao to India, the Chinese Ambassador to Delhi Sun Yuxi had made the outrageous claim that Arunachal Pradesh belonged to China. 'In our position, the whole of what you call the state of Arunachal Pradesh is Chinese territory, and Tawang (district) is only one place in it. We are claiming all of that—that's our position,' he told the news channel *CNN-IBN*. India forced China to call him back. But the events after his return make it amply clear that the Chinese have their eyes firmly set on that state.

For China, the McMahon Line is only an excuse. This so-called 'imperialist line' is the one that demarcates the border between Myanmar and China. It is thus clear that it either intends to occupy more Indian territory or use it as a bargaining chip for something else. The big question is: What could that something else be?

One of the most contentious issues between India and China has been the presence of His Holiness the Dalai Lama and his people on the Indian soil. Although successive Indian governments, starting with Jawaharlal Nehru in 1954, have conceded directly or indirectly that Tibet is a part of China, the Chinese harbour serious apprehensions. They see in His Holiness the Dalai Lama not a venerable saintly figure but a 'divisive politician'. They are convinced that it was His Holiness and the agents of the West that were responsible for the uprising in Tibet and apprehend more trouble in future.

India, on its part, tries to mollycoddle China by assuring it that its soil wouldn't be allowed to be used for any anti-China activities. Yet the suspicions remain. They knew about the tremendous popularity His Holiness the Dalai Lama enjoys in Tibet even to this day despite his exile for almost half-a-century. In the 1980s, when his representatives were allowed by the Chinese authorities to visit Tibet, they received unprecedented and spontaneous welcome. That must have rattled the Chinese leadership.

The Chinese attitude towards the Dalai Lama and his people hardened quite a bit after that, which continues to this day. No effort is spared by China to browbeat countries that extend an invitation to His Holiness the Dalai Lama. It also pressurised Sri Lanka into withdrawing its invitation to him. All this in spite of the fact that countries like India categorically declared that Tibet is an internal matter of China.

This brings us to the most crucial aspect of India-China relations, i.e., the Tibetan exiles including the Dalai Lama, not Tibet. This shift from Tibet to the Tibetans is very important today. For India, the critical issue is its sovereignty. The government has to be firm on that question. The policy of freezing border question and addressing all other issues like bilateral trade and cultural exchanges no longer works. It has to sit down and seriously work on the demarcation of the border by exchanging maps. While doing that we must act as equals, not as subordinates or inferiors.

What plagued Indian establishment was the utter lack of unanimity in the ruling establishment. Reports suggested serious differences between the PMO and the MEA on one side and the Defence Ministry and the Home Ministry on the other.

India has a moral and ethical commitment to His Holiness the Dalai Lama and his people. Every Indian wants them to realise their dream of a return to their homeland but with dignity and honour. India is duty-bound to help in that process. Unfortunately, our government completely abdicated that duty. It is only the US official visitors who raise the question of Tibet with their Chinese counterparts; we seldom do that. Just to reiterate: It is no longer the question of Tibet; it is the question of the Tibetans now.

For almost a decade, the Russia-China talks remained deadlocked over this 'principle' issue. But with the Soviets not budging, the Chinese had to climb down and in 1983, they finally agreed to not insist on the principle anymore. The US and many others tend to dismiss all this as Chinese propaganda. It may be partly true. But the underlying lesson remains; that you don't have to acquire same number of naval carriers as your adversary; you should rather have enough capability to disable them.

'Dialogue is the only solution', our leaders untiringly exhort when it comes to our relations with the neighbours. Undoubtedly. But what is more important is perseverance.

With countries like China, we need to understand that there is no easy solution even if you are ready to talk. The border dispute between our countries is more than six decades old. And the talks too are almost three decades old by now. Not much has been achieved. In fact, while the talks are on, we concede more and achieve little. That is the most important lesson that we must learn: while in talks, be firm. Set your goals firmly before going into the talks; and once there, be steadfast.

Maybe we can take a leaf or two out of China's own history. China resolved a very vexatious border dispute with Russia in 1991. While India has a border stretching to over 4,500 kilometres, Russia too shares a border of almost the same length with China. Interestingly, not just the length of the border but the nature of the dispute too is same. China declares that it doesn't recognise 'imperial treaties' as they were 'unequal' treaties. It is well-known that China wants everything redone after 1949.

The pattern followed by China in its talks with Soviet Russia is similar to what it does with all other countries; and to what it did with India too. When the talks began between China and

Soviet Russia in mid-60s, the Chinese insisted that the Russian side should first of all agree 'on principles'. By 'principles', what it meant was that the Russians should agree with its contention that all the historical treaties arrived at between Russia and China prior to 1949 should be considered as 'unequal treaties'.

Realizing the carefully laid trap in the name of 'principle', the Russians at once rejected the Chinese argument and insisted that they were not going to negotiate a new boundary and were only willing to discuss 'minor technical adjustments'. They accused China of 'attempting to substantiate its claim to 1.5 million square kilometres of land that properly belonged to the Soviet Union by using a far-fetched pretext of righting the "injustices" of past centuries'. Naturally, the initial talks in 1964 collapsed. When they resumed in 1969, the Soviets were firm on their position that there is no question of negotiating a new boundary except to talk about a few issues limited to not more that 0.1 million square kilometres. The Chinese side persisted with its demand that the 'basic principle' of the unequal nature of the past treaties must be accepted by Russia first.

For almost a decade, the Russia-China talks remained deadlocked over this 'principle' issue. But with the Soviets not budging, the Chinese had to climb down and in 1983, they finally agreed to not insist on the principle anymore. Once that happened, the rest of the negotiations went on and a final settlement was arrived at by 1991.

Just to understand the success of Russia and China border settlement we have to understand the mindset of the Russian leaders. One statement of Boris Yeltsin while on his way to Beijing in 1996 would suffice to indicate it: 'There are instances in which we agree to no compromises. For example, the issue of to whom the three islands—in the Amur River, not far from Khabarovsk, and the Bolshoy Island in the Argun River in Chita should belong. With regard to this our position remains firm: the border should be where it lies now.'

Can we show that firmness? Have we done that before? China insisted that it wouldn't recognise McMahon Line since it is an 'Imperial Line'. Have we come across a Yeltsin in India who would have told them that if McMahon Line is fine for China and Burma to settle their borders, why not the same for China and India? Do we have the courage to tell them that barring some 'minor technicalities', the border should be where it lied in 1947 or 1949?

So perseverance—the Russian type, is the key. But two more issues played important role in settling Russia-China border dispute. Firstly, both the countries felt a need for 'coming closer' for strategic purposes. In early 1980s, under Deng Xiaoping, it became an important part of the Chinese new foreign policy. But more importantly, the second factor, the superior military might of Russia, was also a clincher.

No meaningful settlement will be possible between two unequal neighbours. It has been made amply clear by the repeated statements of our military bosses that India lags far behind China in terms of its military capability. Elsewhere the new RSS Sarsanghachalak Shri Mohan Bhagwat also said: 'Though frequent wars and border infringements imposed on us after the independence have made us some what less complacent regarding our defense preparedness, we are still less prepared for any potential war as compared to that of China and it is necessary to make more potent arrangement to secure our borders'.

Critics may call it war-mongering, but the fact remains that we need to strengthen our preparedness. But what do we understand by defense preparedness? Do we mean parity in terms of weapons, aircraft and ships? Is it possible? Someone suggested that since China spends 7 per cent of its GDP on defence, we too should spend that much. But 7 per cent of the GDP for China and 7 per cent of the GDP for India are not the same. Here also, the Chinese experience might give us a clue as to what we should do. For China, the US is a bigger rival. Even to this day, it spends fourteen times more money on its defence than China. China had to face humiliating situation when a US aircraft carrier the USS Nimitz entered the Taiwan Strait in 1995-96 to force China to stand down from its threats to Taiwan. If China learnt any one lesson from this stand-off, it was that in military terms what is important is capability, not necessarily parity. Through capability, one can build deterrents without actually entering into a race for parity. And that is what China did in the last fifteen years.

The Chinese leadership has realised that it would be foolhardy to try to take on the US might head on. Instead, they started working on the stratagem that would give it an advantage in case of any conflict. The bottomline for China is to raise the costs of war exorbitantly high for the US to think several times before taking the plunge. They call the military capabilities that support this strategy as 'assassin's mace'. The 'mantra', to quote the *Foreign Affairs* magazine, is that the 'assassin's mace' will enable 'the inferior' (China) to defeat 'the superior' (the US).

The Chinese today have ICBMs that can effectively destroy forward US bases like the Kadena Air Base on Okinawa Island in Japan or the Anderson Air Force Base on Guam in South of Japan. The message is clear: in the event of war, China has the capability to make the forward bases of the US redundant in no time.

Today, the US is greatly worried about what is described as the 'wasted assets'. It has forward bases, but China has the capability to strike them with accuracy at will. The US has a huge and most powerful Navy, but the Chinese are deploying UAVs, radars and reconnaissance satellites that can detect warships at progressively greater distances. The Chinese have a large number of submarines with advanced torpedoes and high-speed sea-skimming missiles that can stalk US carriers. It has aircraft that carry high-speed anti-ship ballistic missiles. Thus, even the vast US Navy is fast becoming a 'wasted asset' for the US.

In other words, the East Asian seas are a no-go zone for the US Navy today. It is noteworthy that the Chinese Navy is still at its nascent stage. What China did was to demonstrate capability, not necessarily the parity.

Not just the seas and the sky, even the cyberspace is increasingly being made redundant for the US by China. It is reputed to have launched cyber attacks on the Pentagon that disabled computer systems there. Even the low-earth-orbit satellites of the US, which supply crucial military and commercial data for the US, are well within the reach of the anti-satellite ballistic missiles or ground-based lasers of China. Even those are turning out to be a 'wasted asset' for the US. Many of the 'smart weapons' of the US depend on the GPS constellation. The PLA is working overtime to acquire the capability to destroy this constellation thus making the US military just redundant when it comes to any confrontation in the East.

The US and many others tend to dismiss all this as Chinese propaganda. It may be partly true. But the underlying lesson remains that you don't have to acquire same number of naval carriers as your adversary, you should rather have enough capability to disable them. The mute point is: where do we stand in terms of research and production of modern weaponry? Prof. Steve Cohen of the Brookings Institute says that India is the most lethargic country when it comes to indigenous production of weapons. Maybe our politicians and military bosses are driven by 'other' considerations in depending on imports rather than developing indigenously?

Another important lesson that we should learn is to frustrate the enemy. China practices it to the full. It has encircled us from all sides. It has built a 'listening post' in Burma's Coco Islands and upgraded it into a full base later. It has built the Gwadar Port in Sindh, Pakistan. It is building a commercial port in Sri Lanka. It is engaged in building infrastructure in countries like Sri Lanka, Bangladesh and Nepal. All these will become strategic assets for China. The Gwadar port can function as a base for the nuclear submarines of the Chinese Navy.

Sadly, we are doing nothing on that front too. We have done precious little to help countries like Taiwan. Despite the fact that we have best of the relations with Mongolia which is very strategically located: land-locked between Russia and China, we hardly thought of leveraging our relations to the strategic advantage of our country. The argument is that such a move would unnecessarily 'irritate' China. We have an Air Force base in Kazakhstan but no aircraft.

What is needed is a strategic vision, not just statements. Unfortunately, while we seem to lack it, we are not even trying to learn a lesson from our own adversary, China.

52

The Dalai Lama at Eighty-Five

The tiny village of Shaoshan in the Hunan province of China is an important centrepiece of 'Red Tourism'. Busloads of people flock to this birthplace of Mao Zedong to pay their respects to the 'Great Helmsman', whose thirty-six-metre-high statue adorns the village square. There is a Shaoshan Mao Zedong Memorial Museum too, where Mao's belongings are kept.

People are also encouraged to visit the birthplace of Deng Xiaoping in Paifang village of Xiexing Town in the Sichuan province. Although Deng never returned to his village after rising in the communist hierarchy, the Chinese government has made sure that his village also becomes an important destination in Red Tourism. The village was declared by the state council, the Chinese cabinet, in 2001, as a 'Major Historical and Cultural Site Protected at the National Level' and Hu Jintao, the general secretary of the CPC, attended the unveiling of Deng's statue in 2004.

Far removed from these villages, which have become important landmarks in China tourism, is the village of Taktser, in Qinghai province, once a part of the former Tibetan kingdom. Taktser is the birthplace of His Holiness, the fourteenth and the current Dalai Lama. Unlike Shaoshan and Paifang, Taktser does not appear anywhere on the China tourism circuit. The village remains backward, nondescript and forlorn.

'Beijing obviously doesn't want Taktser becoming a pilgrimage site for Tibetans; the Dalai Lama represents a challenge not to Chinese power per se, but to its national(ist) narrative,' writes Tim Robertson, an independent journalist and writer, in *Diplomat* in 2018. What happens if someone, by chance or by effort, visits that village? Robertson narrates his own experience when he made a visit to this village about thirty miles away from Xining, the capital city of the Qinghai province.

In the desolate village, Robertson finally finds an old Tibetan man. 'Looking at me, he asks, "Where are you from?" But before I can answer he turns to my driver and, more alarmed, asks, "Are you Tibetan?" When the driver answers in the affirmative, the villager—with an obvious sense of urgency—tells us to leave quickly because the place is heavily surveilled. His voice is foreboding and his jerky, hurried gestures make it clear that this is not a place to loiter,' he writes.

Incidentally, I too had a similar experience when I visited this village ten years before Robertson. At that time, I was probably one of the very few Indians who had visited the birthplace of His Holiness. I was on a tour of China in November 2008, and my itinerary included a visit to Lhasa. The hosts, a wing of the CPC, saw the controlled visit as an opportunity to showcase the progress and development of the Tibetan Autonomous Region (TAR) under the CPC regime. The visit to Lhasa was to start from Xining, where I was made to board the train service of the Qinghai-Tibet Railways. The twenty-six-hour train journey was a memorable one. The train practically runs on a glacier, and doubtless, is a technological marvel.

But the most memorable part of the trip was my impromptu visit to Taktser. His Holiness is loved by six million Tibetans. One of them informed me in Xining about the village which was only ninety minutes away. My protocol officer, an official from the CPC, was obviously uncomfortable. He pleaded helplessness as it was not a part of the itinerary provided. But I could persuade him for a quick evening visit to that village. Few miles from the city, roads were bad, and by Chinese standards, they can be described as non-existent. It was obvious that the village and its surroundings were subject to deliberate neglect and disinterest.

When I visited the house where His Holiness was born, I was greeted by a close relative, who took me around. There was no electricity and hence the house was lit by a generator. There was a room with a bed for His Holiness to retire and another bigger room with an elevated podium in Tibetan style for him to give *darshan* and discourses. Both the rooms were beautifully decorated. 'Do you hope to have him back here?' I asked in part surprise and part bewilderment. His Holiness's nephew was affirmative. I realised that this hope is what drives the six million Tibetans in preserving their religion, language and culture against heavy odds.

His Holiness had left Lhasa in 1959 and ended up in India as a refugee. Over 80,000 Tibetans followed him subsequently. The expatriate Tibetan community is about 1,50,000 today. He was received by Jawaharlal Nehru and granted asylum in India. His Holiness and his followers have since been staying mainly in Dharamshala and also at a few other places like Uttarakhand, Darjeeling, Mainpat in Chhattisgarh and Mundgod in Karnataka, where they were provided land by the Indian Government for their livelihood.

However, this asylum issue was preceded by a lot of drama. Once before, in 1957, His Holiness was invited for the Mahaparinirvana—2,500 years of the Buddha's nirvana—celebrations at Bodh Gaya. His Holiness came with an entourage and mind to use the occasion to seek political asylum in India or the US. The two brothers of the Dalai Lama, who were already sanctioned asylum by the US, came down to meet him in India. However, Nehru and Zhou Enlai had left no stone unturned to ensure that His Holiness returned to Tibet. Zhou Enlai had stayed for full twelve days in India to make sure that the Dalai Lama did not stay back in India. Ultimately, the Dalai Lama had returned to Lhasa in early 1958, only to return in a year's time.

Nehru, although agreed to grant asylum to His Holiness this time, was not sure whether he had done the right thing. India was never there to support the Tibetan cause during the fateful years of the 1950s despite repeated requests by the Dalai Lama for support at the UN. Tunku Abdul Rahman, the prime minister of Malaysia, was flabbergasted by India's reluctance to support the Tibetan cause and sorely complained that, 'Twice Malaya raised the Tibetan question in the UNO and twice India refused to support us … we knew what was going to happen when China took Tibet. They had their eyes on India and wanted to get nearer to your borders.'

Even the Dalai Lama had cautioned Nehru about the same and said, 'If you deny sovereign status to Tibet, you deny the validity of the convention, and therefore, the validity of the McMahon Line.' Instead of making sense of the Dalai Lama's caution, Nehru got angry with the statement. 'What good will it achieve?' was Nehru's rhetoric when asked for the support to the Tibetan cause at the UN in the 1950s.

Nehru always held the view that Tibet was an integral part of China. In an interview to R.K. Karanjia in 1954, Nehru categorically stated, 'Tibet, of course, is part of China.' He also said on another occasion that the Chinese occupation of Tibet would put an end to the theocratic regime of the priestly lamas and bring it into 'the mainstream of modern civilisation'.

Speaking a few months after the arrival of the Dalai Lama in India in the Rajya Sabha in October 1959, Nehru wryly said, 'Very probably, the Tibetan developments have angered and soured the minds of the government in China, very likely ... And perhaps, they have reacted strongly to what we have done, I mean, to the asylum we have given to the Dalai Lama.'

His Holiness has remained in India ever since. He has completed sixty-one years of living in India. When he came, he was a refugee. But today, every Indian regards him as an elder in the family. His Holiness jovially says that while his body was Tibetan, his blood was Indian since he has been eating the rice and dal of this country for so many decades. He is as much a revered spiritual master to Indians as he has been to many Tibetans and others. His Holiness has regarded Hinduism and Buddhism as twins, following identical paths, one with the conception of *Atma* and the other with *Anatma*.

Once he narrated to me his conversation with Prime Minister Morarji Desai: 'We are two branches of the same tree of Dharma,' Desai told His Holiness, to which His Holiness promptly responded saying, 'You are the tree, and we are the branches.'

This humility is the hallmark of His Holiness. In fact, at Emory University, where he was an honorary professor, His Holiness has described the essence of his philosophy in four words—humility, honesty, transparency and compassion. His Holiness is the living manifestation of these supreme qualities. Compassion, the essence of Buddhism, has taken a human form in His Holiness; he is compassion-incarnate.

53

COVID-19 and the Contours of the New World Order

The world is grappling with the coronavirus pandemic. People are dying in large numbers. Healthcare and the economy are under severe stress. Countries are turning inwards, closing borders, to protect their people. As historian Yuval Noah Harari wrote, more and more countries are becoming nationalist and protectionist, even, in some cases, authoritarian.

But the coronavirus disease has taught us a different lesson, a lesson of interdependence. The pandemic is global. The battle to combat it too must be global. We depend on each other for our healthcare equipment, services, transportation facilities, and, finally the vaccines, as and when they are invented. India has imported masks and testing kits from some countries, while exporting critical drugs such as hydroxychloroquine to many countries, including the United States. Global supply chains have become critical not only for healthcare products, but also for food and other supplies.

In fact, one big realisation for countries from the pandemic has been that nationalism of the closed kind won't work. Donald Trump's 'America first' nationalism didn't work. He had to turn to China, India, and South Korea for supplies. A recurring theme of many a political scientist about American exceptionalism stands shattered today. Isolationists in all countries, including India, must realise that post-COVID-19 world will be more integrationist than isolationist.

For some time now, it has become a fad with political scientists to talk about multi-polarity. But the 21st-century world is no longer being led by countries alone. We have corporations that have bigger GDPs than many countries in the world. We have players outside the State that wield enormous influence on people across national boundaries. More important, in the era of social media, a number of power groups have emerged in the world that defy national boundaries. While nationalism as a political ideology is making a return, the world is also slipping into what author Parag Khanna has described as hetero-polarity. It may be premature to predict the post-COVID-19 world order, but it can conclusively be said that we are moving into a hetero-polar world, with multiple State and non-State power players actively crisscrossing each other's paths.

Prime Minister Narendra Modi has to lead India into that world after the pandemic. Modi described the situation as 'World War-like'. That has catalysed the building of a narrative around Second World War. Comparisons are being drawn between Modi and Franklin D. Roosevelt, who led the US into WWII.

Incidentally, both Roosevelt and Adolf Hitler came to power in the US and Germany respectively in the same year (1932). While Hitler turned into a despot, subjecting European neighbours to domination and aggression, Roosevelt focused on rebuilding the US. His 'New Deal' led to massive infrastructure building, such as highways, bridges and railways in the US, and helped the country come out of the Great Depression of the 1930s. Expectations are that Modi will also do something similar.

Japan's bombing of Pearl Harbor in December 1941 forced Roosevelt into the war. By the end of the war in 1945, the US emerged as the leading world power replacing Great Britain. But Roosevelt's contribution to the War was not just about the defeat of the Axis powers. Roosevelt was instrumental in building two global institutions. Through the Bretton Woods Conference in 1944, he laid the foundation for the World Bank and International Monetary Fund. The US dollar emerged as the global currency. In April 1945, the United Nations Organization (UNO) was born with the US and its allies in the driver's seat.

At a time when this post-COVID-19 world order appears to be in disarray, it will be tempting to expect Modi to don the Rooseveltian mantle and take the lead in building new global institutions. Institutions of the WWII vintage such as the World Health Organization and United Nations Security Council have become overtly partisan and lost their credibility today. 'The United Nations is far less credible today than it has been through its history,' S. Jaishankar, India's external affairs minister said recently. With the US facing its worst nightmare, and the credibility of the Chinese leadership at an all-time low, the presumption that Modi should step into the role that Roosevelt played seventy-five years ago sounds logical.

Perhaps, Modi should go back, not seventy-five years, but by a century, and look at the role Woodrow Wilson had played at the end of First World War. 'Wilson saw America's mission in First World War not as material aggrandisement but as leading all nations into a new international community organised to achieve right ends,' wrote political scientist Joseph Nye. Wilson's famous

14-point charter for world peace, outlined in his address to the US Congress in January 1918, underscores the moral leadership of the US.

Wilsonianism of the 20th century was represented by liberal internationalism, democracy, non-intervention, collective security and humanitarian cooperation. In the last six years, Modi has shown his commitment to all these political ideals. In fact, during his COVID-19 consultations with the G20 and South Asian Association for Regional Cooperation partners, he presented his model centred on humanism as 'human-centric development cooperation'.

Modi-ism of the post-COVID 21st-century world can be borne out of the democratic and humanist credentials that he has displayed in the fight against COVID-19.

Acknowledgements

The Spirit of Democracy

1. *The Art of the Possible* was originally published in *Open* on 6 November 2018.
2. *A Study in Greatness* was originally published in the web exclusives of *Open* on 1 October 2018.
3. *On Gandhi and Gandhism* was reproduced from the text of an address at the Mount Carmel College, Bengaluru on 26 November 2019 and was originally published in *Open* on 30 November 2019.
4. *The Beauty of Indic Thought* was adapted from the author's inaugural address on 17 December 2017 at the Indic Thought Festival held in Goa. Originally published in *Open* on 22 December 2017.
5. *Three Warnings of B.R. Ambedkar* was originally published in the web exclusives of *Open* on 6 December 2018.
6. *Cultivating Constitutional Morality* was originally published in *Open* on 26 November 2019.
7. *Samajik Samrasta (Social Harmony): Shri Guruji M.S. Golwalkar* was written in 2008 during the birth centenary celebrations of the second Sarsanghachalak of the RSS PP Shri Guruji, M.S. Golwalkar and published on the author's blog.

8. *Deendayal Upadhyaya: The Swayamsewak* was originally published in the *Indian Express* on 25 September 2019.
9. *Betrayal of the Mahatama* was originally published in the *Indian Express* on 30 January 2019.
10. *A Need for Vigilance* was originally published in the *Indian Express* on 30 June 2015.

Confronting History

11. *Correcting a Historic Blunder* was originally published in the *Indian Express* on 6 August 2019.
12. *The End of Victimhood Politics* was originally published in *Open* on 20 September 2019.
13. *Kashmir is Ours, Also Means That Every Kashmiri is Ours* was originally published in the *Indian Express* on 26 February 2019.
14. *Are Gupkaris Listening?* was originally published in the *Greater Kashmir* on 7 September 2020.
15. *A Time for New Leaders* was originally published in the *Indian Express* on 22 August 2019.
16. *The Supremacy of the Indian State and Parliament* was originally published in *Hindustan Times* on 6 August 2019.
17. *Roots and Rights in Assam after NRC* was originally published in *Open* on 14 September 2018.
18. *A Different Leader* was originally published in the *Indian Express* on 30 September 2016.
19. *A People's Idea* was originally published in the *Indian Express* on 29 December 2015.
20. *Strategic Culture* was originally published on the author's blog on 21 November 2012.

A View from Within

21. *Gentle, Yet Atal* was excerpted from the first 'Atal Bihari Vajpayee Memorial Lecture' delivered by the author at Thinkers Forum, Bengaluru on 17 December 2018. The article was originally published in *Organiser* on 25 December 2018.
22. *In Atalji's Mould* was originally published in the *Indian Express* on 27 August 2019.
23. *Election Result: In Favour of Narendra Modi* first appeared in the print edition of the *Indian Express* on 24 May 2019 as *The Leader is the Truth*.
24. *Glasnost in RSS* was originally published in the *Indian Express* on 25 September 2018.
25. *Leader, Cadre, Parivar* was originally published in the *Indian Express* on 6 April 2018.
26. *Ram Mandir Movement: A One-Way Street for BJP* was originally published in the *Indian Express* on 6 December 2017.
27. *Somnath to Ayodhya: Journey of an Awakened Civilisation* was originally published on *Chintan—India Foundation blogs* on 5 August 2020.
28. Ayodhya is for Ayuddha: Non-War and Peace Communities was originally published in the *Economic Times* on 8 August 2020.
29. *In Sita's Footsteps* was originally published in *Open* on 2 May 2020.
30. *Despite the People* was originally published in the *Indian Express* on 24 November 2018.
31. *After Empowerment, Freedom and Dignity* was originally published in the *Indian Express* on 8 March 2019.

32. *Because India Comes First* was originally published in the *Indian Express* on 17 May 2014.

Facing the Facts

33. *Liberal Fascists* was originally published on the author's blog on 2 August 2011.
34. *Know Your Terrorist* was originally published on the author's blog on 17 July 2011.
35. *Citizenship Act: For Persecuted Minorities* originally published in *Open* on 1 January 2020.
36. *At the Root of Today's Crisis, an Intellectual Void* was originally published in *Hindustan Times* on 30 July 2020.
37. *Our Lives Matter* was originally published in *Open* on 17 June 2020.
38. *Soft Power Struggles* was originally published on *Chintan—India Foundation Blogs* on 23 July 2020.
39. *Challenges to Global Governance* was originally published in the *Sunday Guardian* on 6 July 2020.
40. *When Democracy was Unshackled* was originally published in the *Indian Express* on 25 June 2020.

India and the World

41. *Shalom Al Yisrael* was originally published in *Open* on 10 May 2019.
42. *Look beyond Transactionalism* was originally published in the *Times of India Blogs* on 16 April 2018.
43. *Maa Ganga by Another Name* was originally published in *Open* on 23 March 2018.
44. *The Meaning of De-hyphenation* was originally published in the *Indian Express* on 11 July 2017.

45. *Turning down China* was originally published in the *Indian Express* on 27 May 2017.
46. *New India, Different China* was originally published in the *Indian Express* on 13 April 2017.
47. *Wolf Warrior Diplomacy* was originally published in the *Indian Express* on 4 June 2020.
48. *The Heat in Beijing* was originally published in *Open* on 22 May 2020.
49. *Going beyond Panchsheel* was originally published in the *Indian Express* on 28 June 2014.
50. *China: The Real Foreign Policy Challenge for India* was originally published in the *Indian Express* on 7 June 2014.
51. *India has a Moral Commitment on Tibet* was originally published in *Organiser* in two parts on 4 October and 11 October 2009.
52. *The Dalai Lama at Eighty-Five* was originally published in *Open* on 5 July 2020.
53. *COVID-19 and the Contours of the New World Order* was originally published in *Hindustan Times* on 14 April 2020.

www.ingramcontent.com/pod-product-compliance
Lightning Source LLC
Chambersburg PA
CBHW020832160426
43192CB00007B/614